ADVANCED DRESSAGE

ANTHONY CROSSLEY

ADVANCED DRESSAGE

ANTHONY CROSSLEY

SWAN·HILL

PRESS

Copyright © 1982, 1995 by Executors of the late Anthony Crossley

This edition first published in the UK in 1995
by Swan Hill Press, an imprint of Airlife Publishing Ltd.
Previously first published by Stanley Paul and Co. Ltd., 1982

British Library Cataloguing in Publication Data
A catalogue record for this book
is available from the British Library

ISBN 1 85310 707 7

Printed in England by Livesey Ltd., Shrewsbury.

Swan Hill Press
an imprint of Airlife Publishing Ltd.
101 Longden Road, Shrewsbury SY3 9EB, England

Frontispiece: *Christine Stuckelberger on Granat*

Contents

List of Illustrations

Line drawings

The author is deeply indebted to Hugo Czerny, Werner Ernst, Neil ffrench-Blake, Leslie Lane, John Minoprio, Jim Bennett, John Bunting and Anthony Loriston-Clarke for the many excellent action photographs that grace and embellish this book.

Foreword

by Dr Reiner Klimke

I have known Anthony Crossley as a journalist, critic and rider since the time when I was riding my World Champion dressage horse Mehmed. Our acquaintance grew into an equestrian friendship when, after the Olympic Games at Montreal in 1976, he came to us as our guest at Munster in order to watch the training of our horses. By riding one or two of them he was able to feel for himself much of what he could see of the daily work.

Advanced Dressage is the result of the author's experience as a rider as well as a journalist. What appeals to me personally is its clear structure and the description of the individual stages of the development of the horse and rider. Thanks to this, the reader can easily look up whatever problem is concerning him at any time and find sound advice about it.

The author has had the courage to include in the book certain pictures that show what may need to be done in day-to-day work as temporary exercises, rather than showing only the ideal form of movement. For example, the two photographs on pages 38 and 39, which illustrate the theme of 'long and deep', show the horse's nose behind the vertical where it is not ideally supposed to be. But these photographs must be studied in the context of their captions and of the main text where it is made clear that the purpose of this valuable exercise is to loosen and strengthen the all-important muscles of the horse's back.

I am glad to find the author expressing the opinion that the development of the canter pirouette should start from the shoulder-in position rather than from the travers. That opinion deserves support because only in that way will the horse remain straight, in a light position, and bending in the direction he is going. Colonel de Heux from Holland has already given a similar warning.

Training a dressage horse is a protracted and difficult process. The author's merit lies in the fact that he has described that process up to the most advanced stages in a way that is so clear and easy to understand.

Preface

This book is written as a sequel to *Training the Young Horse – the First Two Years*. The purpose of the earlier book was to help riders of only modest experience to organize the basic training of an all-purpose riding horse and to educate the horse in all the simple but desirable qualities of balance, impulsion, some degree of collection, suppleness, obedience and activity. The schedule included simple lateral movements and flying changes in canter – all to be achieved within approximately twenty-four months from the time the unbroken horse is first taken in hand. Given the right guidelines, those standards, which amount to Medium standard dressage, are within the capabilities of most riders and most horses, subject only to the possession of a stable and supple seat by the rider and to the availability of adequate, though inexpensive, working facilities. *The First Two Years* was also written in the hope that it would encourage riders to raise the standards of accomplishment that they were accustomed to demand of themselves and of their horses, without necessarily entering the sphere of specialized dressage. It aimed at a standard of intelligent pleasure for those who might never wish to become involved in all the rigours of advanced dressage.

But there will always be those who wish to develop their equestrian studies further, beyond the point of general utility and simple riding comfort. It is for riders with such ambitions that this second book is written, to help them make some advance into the realms of higher equitation and to give them confidence to tackle, with their horses, at least some and possibly all the training movements contained in the curricula for the internationally established Prix St Georges, the two Intermediaires and the Grand Prix de Dressage tests.

The work covered in this book requires an intensive, thoughtful and specialized approach. That is not to say that a horse undergoing advanced dressage training should never be used for other purposes. Indeed – and just because this advanced work will greatly improve his gymnastic ability – he should, as a result of such training, be able to function better in other spheres such as hunting, eventing or jumping. Nevertheless, some degree of specialization must be accepted, if only because without it progress would be so slow as to defeat its own ends. The exercises and targets become increasingly demanding and difficult for the horse, as for the rider, so that, unless both parties are willing and able to concentrate for regular and prolonged periods on mastering the many subtle and intricate problems involved, they are likely to find themselves becoming frustrated and, eventually, bored or depressed. Advanced dressage is therefore not for everyone, though it is, up to limits that will vary with the character and talent of each rider, a perfectly practical proposition for a great many more people than have ever been tempted to practise it in the past in Great Britain.

No book, while remaining readable, can possibly cover all the special circumstances and problems that a rider is likely to encounter when trying to teach himself and his horse to perform a whole sequence of gymnastic movements that may sound, when described on paper, relatively simple. The potential variations in behaviour that exist in the two living partners, due to idiosyncrasies of character, physical and mental stress, misunder-standings and plain but honest clumsiness, make any comprehensive catalogue of those problems virtually impossible to compile. There is therefore no reliable substitute for a combination of intensive reading from the works of past masters and of frequent assistance and advice from an experienced trainer – be he friend, spouse or professional – throughout the whole training process. Without guidance from the ground, and even perhaps with it, every rider will fall far short of his own ideals with the first horse he tries to train. In other words, he will, somewhere along the line, spoil the first horse, and will in all probability do the same, albeit to a progressively lesser extent, with the second and third. He should not be ashamed of that sombre thought, for it has been the experience of all those who have gone before him. All dressage riders learn from the doing of it and, since every single horse is psychologically and physically different, it is impossible for anyone to learn it all. By the same token, the more the rider rides, the more he learns. It is also a fact, paradoxically, that all thinking riders come, sooner or later, to realize that the greater their experience, the more they appreciate the inadequacies of their knowledge.

I have tried particularly in this book to disentangle and analyse the main principles that run like golden threads through the whole of dressage from its earliest stages to its highest development in the high school work. Advanced dressage is not a world by itself. It is merely a straightforward and logical progression in which the same principal threads form infallible guides – if we do not lose or distort them. If I have been successful in making those threads easier to recognize and to follow, I shall have achieved my purpose.

I am acutely aware of the limitations of my own experience, and consequently of my understanding, of advanced dressage. I can claim, however, to know a little about some of the answers. To that claim I will add the belief that my experience and knowledge, such as it is, has been soundly based and is fit to be offered, with humility, to others. So, to all those riders who enjoy training horses and want to increase their knowledge and experience, I advocate courage and *Advanced Dressage* and the adoption of the motto 'To have got part way is better than not to have started.'

Introduction

This book, like its predecessor, is divided into two parts. Part One deals with general principles that need to be firmly established in the mind of the trainer of an advanced dressage horse. To some extent, this section will amount to a recapitulation, but it is also an elaboration, of the equivalent section of the previous book. Its purpose is to make possible the avoidance of subsequent reiteration of a number of facets of riding that will be of recurrent importance throughout the whole process of the work that lies ahead.

Part Two will consist of a series of relatively short essays, or chapters, each dealing with one specific movement or aspect of advanced dressage. The order in which the chapter subjects are presented must not be taken as a firm recommendation of the order in which they should be given priority in training. Some guidance on that score will be found at appropriate places within the chapters, but generally speaking the logic of the movement sequences that guided us so clearly through *The First Two Years* is no longer relevant. Most of the more advanced movements dealt with in this book tend to complement rather than to evolve from each other, and are therefore not subject to the same sequence discipline.

Training sequences

The order in which chapter subjects are introduced will be governed largely by the principle that all lessons will be leading us in the same direction, towards the same ultimate goal, and that in every case the easiest one should be taught and mastered first. The sequence adopted must therefore be logical from the point of view of the severity of the physical demands that each lesson will make on the horse, and in that way the chapters will be roughly in keeping with the development of the standard international dressage tests. In practice, however, it is possible that the trainer will find himself, quite logically, developing several lines of progress simultaneously. For example, the development of flying changes down to one-time has no direct bearing on the development of canter pirouettes which themselves evolve from lateral work. The development of both exercises can therefore proceed in parallel, and this is a good example of why it is neither necessary nor practical to try to lay down a precise and arbitrary sequence. It often happens that the problem of what to work on next will resolve itself as time goes on, the horse becoming more and more confidently accomplished until he almost offers to 'have a go' at a more difficult exercise. Conversely, if the next movement is clearly presenting difficulty, the trainer can be sure that the preparation and the performance of the previous and easier work has not been sufficient. In that case the new exercise should be postponed for the time being.

Part One

I

General Guidance

The time factor

One big difference in the approach to overall training for advanced dressage, as compared with those first two years, is that there will be no clear-cut, precisely timed schedule. The work that has to be undertaken is too difficult and the potential achievements too uncertain to make any such schedule a practical proposition. We are entering a stage of equitation which may become a lifetime's study, and we have to be prepared to wait and see how we get on. The successive targets become more formidable, and progress must consequently be slower. As in mountaineering, the higher the peak to be climbed, the more vital it is to establish firmly each successive foothold. There is too much at risk from a careless mistake or miscalculated decision.

We must not, however, assume that time is of no importance. There comes a moment with all living things when they pass the peak of their ability to develop their talents. Significantly, most of them reach that peak when they are relatively young, before the rough and tumble of life has begun to take its mental and physical toll. It follows that, while taking care not to be precipitate, we must make haste while the going is good. To use the analogy of the mountaineers again, we want to reach the top before it gets dark and while there is still time to enjoy the view.

Speed of progress

Despite our hesitations about using a rigorous time schedule for our advanced dressage programme, we can perhaps usefully suggest a minimum and a maximum time over which the work envisaged may profitably be spread. With regard to the minimum period and bearing in mind the relative inexperience of the riders to whom this book is primarily addressed, it would not be reasonable to suppose that the full scope of the curriculum – that is to say, all the movements normally required for the Grand Prix de Dressage test – could be mastered with a modest degree of competence in less than six or seven years from the time the horse was first backed, or four or five years after a satisfactory completion of those first two years of basic training. The very talented and experienced rider with first-rate working facilities would naturally make much better progress and would probably think in terms of about five years overall after backing. But such people belong to a very exclusive group, with probably half a dozen Grand Prix horses to their credit.

But, even for the most talented riders, progress is not always smooth and easy. Questions of temperament or physique may well create problems of much greater significance than are likely to occur in the earlier years of simpler work. These may seriously delay or even prohibit progress in certain directions – the piaffe and passage being obvious examples of movements that not every horse is capable of mastering. And there are others which, possibly as the result of faulty or insufficient preparatory training, may take years to bring up to a satisfactory standard. That is another reason why the wise trainer will make haste while he can and, if only because of the obvious advantages of making good use of the horse's youth, we should never deliberately aim to stretch the advanced training over more years than we need. The horse will certainly learn quicker when he is relatively young and there will then be more years in which the rider will be able to enjoy the fruits of his labours.

Apart from those very practical points of view, we need not be unduly worried about the question of maximum training time. Most horses are capable of continuing to make some improvement for as long as they retain a reasonably supple and sound physique and a happy mental outlook. If the trainer has taken care to preserve those qualities in his mount, he can continue to extend their mutual education until at least the later part of the second decade of the horse's life. Even then, if the horse remains regularly in work, there could be several more years of mutual pleasure extending into the horse's third decade, though by that time he would almost certainly be out of place in serious competitions.

Past, present and future

Each rider's vision and thoughts about the advanced training of his horse should have at their core an acute and constant awareness of the essential

a

b

Two very different types. (a) The grey, Peter Jones (16:2½), an unusual and difficult type for advanced dressage, but a master of pirouettes and one-time changes. (b) A pure thoroughbred, Burak (16:3), well balanced conformation, calm temperament, light but very difficult for pirouettes link between the work done yesterday or today and the ultimate result hoped for in a year or so's time. This link must always be in the forefront of his mind during every exercise he is working on, becoming ever clearer as the work becomes more advanced and the ultimate aim comes into sight. More and more we discover that the advanced work consists mainly of intricate variations on the originally simple themes. In some cases two themes are blended together, as with the counter-change-of-hand in canter where the half-passes are linked directly with flying changes. In others, the original theme is taken to the ultimate, as when the single flying change that originally caused us so much trouble and anxiety is refined to the point when it can be performed without effort at each and every successive stride; or when the simple half-pass, originally performed on an easy diagonal, is collected and controlled until it can, in the form of a pirouette, be performed at the canter on a tiny circle of less than the horse's length in diameter.

In dealing with studies of that or similar nature, we have to be prepared to think in terms of years rather than months. To bring them to their full perfection we must strive patiently until we arrive at our goal, trying at all costs to avoid making a hasty or false step.

The keynote

If it were possible to compress into a few short sentences a keynote theme for our assault on the higher flights of dressage training, it might well be to stress the ever-increasing need to tighten up on the discipline of perfection in all aspects of our work, down to the smallest detail, for horse and for rider, and particularly for the latter. Check and re-check. Polish and perfect. Only the best that you are capable of is of any lasting interest. The rider will by this time know all the essential rules and theories and he must never make excuses if he fails to abide by them. He must go back and do it again, and again, until it comes good. He must stop trying to make progress with his horse – if necessary for several weeks – while he makes some permanent correction to a fault in his own riding technique of which he has become aware. In this latter respect, he must all the time, and always, be asking himself the question: 'How can I ride better?' He must then accept no excuses for failing to improve himself.

2

Preparations for the Rider

The need for the rider to take very seriously his own proficiency as a horseman, as well as his practical and moral obligations to his horse, was described at length in Part One of *The First Two Years*. Its importance is even greater at this advanced stage, and it is therefore worthwhile to elaborate here on certain aspects of the rider's role. For, when all is said and done, it is the skill and talent of the rider, rather than of the horse, that determines the result of any dressage programme. It is the rider's skill, not the horse's, that is exposed, for better or worse, in a dressage display or competition. If the result shows failure, it will rightly be the rider's horsemanship and his lack of skill as a trainer that will be judged at fault. It follows that his own proficiency must be every rider's primary and perpetual concern, and he will be wise constantly to remind himself that, if his horse has not learnt, then he himself has not taught. That has to be accepted as the ultimate answer to virtually everything that a horse does not do well.

Books and knowledge

The rider with little or no previous experience of advanced dressage will find himself launched on a journey during which he will be beset by many puzzling and frustrating problems. There will always be a risk that he will fail to overcome satisfactorily at least some of those problems and that he will have to admit defeat on certain aspects of his project. To minimize that risk, he would be less than sensible if he did not take every possible precaution to brief himself beforehand with all the available information about the topography of the route he is to follow. Fortunately, this information is at hand in the form of books written by those who have made the journey before and have arrived more or less intact at the destination. No one book will contain all the information that our traveller will require, but that has its advantages, since each writer will express himself in his own individual manner, influenced by his unique personal experience. Even if two writers agree in principle about a certain matter, the fact that they have a different way of expressing themselves may be a help to the reader in obtaining clarification of the essence of a problem. He may more easily understand the meaning of one method of phraseology than another.

Every intelligent dressage rider should read carefully and thoughtfully the best books available on the subject. Furthermore he should own rather than borrow those books so that they will be readily at hand for re-reading or for checking on small points at frequent intervals. For most of us, there is no substitute for this reading. It is the only way we have of obtaining a relatively comprehensive knowledge of our subject in time to avoid spoiling our chances of achieving modest success with our horses.

In almost all these books – and there are not so very many of them – the information contained is so closely packed, and at the same time so vitally important, that it is almost impossible to remember it all after just one reading. In many instances, the full implications of a statement may only become apparent when the rider, perhaps some months later, actually experiences the problem during the training of his own horse. That will be the moment to refer back to the book, or perhaps to several books, to refresh the memory on what exactly the masters had to say on the subject. In short, books are for reading, not for lying on bookshelves. And from where else can a rider obtain quick access to the experience of decades and even of centuries? A short list of recommended books is given in an appendix to this book.

Previous experience

In order to reduce the disadvantages arising from the lack of previous experience of the rider in the exercises he will be trying to carry out, it is advisable to make a very detailed study of the technicalities of each new movement some considerable time before that movement is tackled for the first time in the schooling arena. It is no use, for example, suddenly deciding, without any mental preparation, to go out one morning and begin to teach the horse the canter pirouette. Long before that day, the rider should have made it his business to watch many, many pirouettes being performed by other riders, both good and bad. He should have thought out all the details of exactly what the horse has to do at all stages of the movement, as well as exactly what the rider must do to help and encourage the horse to overcome the problems of performing a totally new and very difficult movement. He should have thought out the equine mechanics involved – that is to say, the interaction and interrelation of every part of the horse's anatomy. He should have discussed with other people the problems likely to be encountered and the various ways of approaching them. And in all this common-sense investigation he will be greatly helped if, as suggested in the previous paragraphs, he has read and thought about, and re-read, the appropriate sections of all the authoritative books. If the rider sincerely practises this sort of approach to his task, he is unlikely to find any part of it altogether too difficult for him. He will have built up a well-founded confidence, based on thoroughly sound knowledge, and will be able to take each new step in his stride at the appropriate time. He will know his subject and that is halfway to success. But if he does not take these precautions his clumsy unpreparedness is likely to cause irretrievable damage to his project.

Riding essentials

Every detail of what is required of a dressage rider, as universally agreed by the authors of the great books and by those that have compiled the FEI Rules for Dressage, must be accepted at its face value as vital to success. Those essentials are oulined most briefly in the FEI Rules. The hands, the arms, the elbows, the seat, the legs are all covered, and further elaboration can easily be found in the other books. These matters – some of which may at first glance appear trivial to the self-opinionated or to the sceptical – are in reality each of them of great importance. Properly executed and co-ordinated, they produce a good horseman. Take one of them away, and the rider is no longer all of a piece. He is flawed, and his horse will assuredly also become flawed. Under no circumstances can the rider afford to neglect even one of the numerous criteria. He must concern himself with all of them.

The seat

The rider's seat is the beginning and the end of all his problems. Being the foundation of all the aids, it forms the basis of the rider's alphabet of communication with his horse. With his seat he teaches, he corrects, he

The rider must be able to retain a still and supple seat, however big or strong the horse's movement. Note especially the still lower leg on the girth. Reiner Klimke on Notturno

makes demands and he controls. In this way, the use of the legs, the application of the reins through the hands, and the contact and influence of the actual seat itself become one and indivisible.

We are going to be talking about a very specialized business. Its techniques are based on fine tolerances in which there is no longer any room for half-measures or for any lack of self-discipline. We cannot hope to make even reasonably satisfactory progress unless our seat, our chief and most powerful tool, is a good one. What, then, is a good seat?

Before attempting to answer that question, we should remind ourselves of an important principle. In order to enable our horse to enjoy

Figure 1 *The mechanics and the influence of the seat*

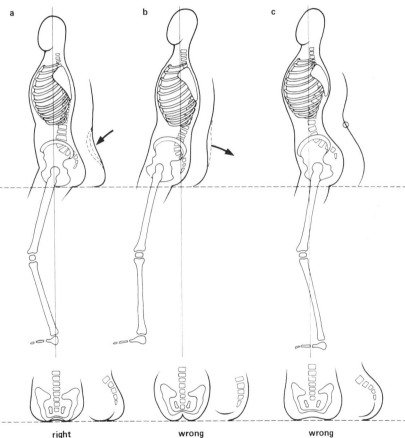

right	wrong	wrong
1. upright	1. leaning back	1. weight in front of seat bones
2. top of pelvis pushed forward	2. pelvis tipped back	2. no action in small of back
3. forward action in small of the back and hip bones	3. buttocks closed and high	3. no contact with seat bones
4. weight carried down with forward influence	4. backward drag in small of the back	4. no forward influence
5. buttocks open and low	5. buttocks tucked under	
6. lower spine effective as shock-absorber	6. incorrect bracing	
	7. no forward influence	
	8. spine unable to act as shock-absorber	

himself while pleasing us – a difficult enough requirement in all conscience – we have to ensure that we sit on his back in such a way that we cause him the minimum of inconvenience and discomfort, but without sacrificing our ability to exert the maximum degree of influence over his actions. Within that context, the logical conclusion must be that the greater the influence of the seat itself in the saddle, the less it will be necessary to inconvenience the horse with the potentially more disturbing actions of reins, legs, bit and spurs. Hence the overriding importance of developing the rider's seat.

First, the rider must place himself in the saddle as nearly as possible over the centre of balance of the horse and in such a way that he is himself in perfect balance without the need of any form of grip or muscular contraction. To combine these two aspects he must primarily sit as close to the pummel of the saddle as he can comfortably manage, and of course that involves the selection of an intelligently designed saddle. In addition, he has to ensure that the weight of his head and torso is placed in balance directly above the only firm base on which he can support himself – namely, the two bones at the bottom of his pelvis that we call the seatbones. He should sit on these as though he were perched on a narrow plank over an abyss, from which he might quite easily fall, but with nothing to grip between his knees. To achieve this balance, he will need to sit up rather straight, pushing slightly forward the top of the pelvis so as to place all parts of the upper body in correct alignment over the seatbones. Then he must sit still. In that dangerous position over the abyss, no excuses will be allowed: no lolling head; no drooping shoulders; no waving elbows. He must sit up, poised and still, because his life depends on it, and he must do the same on the horse because the animal's comfort, and consequently his gymnastic ability, also depends on it.

In making the slight movement of the pelvis to obtain the best possible posture, it is important to remember that it is not the seatbones but the top of the pelvis that moves forward. Once the rider sits down on the correct spot on the saddle, the seatbones have little to do in the more simple movements except to form the bearing point for the weight of the body and to act as the pivot over which the top of the pelvis is gently rocked, to and fro, as may be necessary to correct the balance, to follow the forward movement of the horse and to absorb bumps. The rocking movement is very slight, but it is there and it is of vital importance.

The legs

The legs hang down, relaxed and quite still, in a perfectly natural position from the knee down – a position that is dictated solely by gravity acting on the shape and weight of the boot-encased leg and foot. The length and weight of the foot, positioned as it is in front of the shinbone, will ensure, without any conscious effort, that the lower leg aligns itself a little behind the vertical. We must not allow the feet to turn out, as this tends to produce an inward contraction of the muscles of the upper thighs and buttocks which will draw those muscles inwards and underneath the seatbones, lifting them off the saddle and destroying that vital point of contact and communication. An out-turned foot also means an out-turned knee and that in turn restricts the rider's ability to make the slight backward and forward adjustments of his lower leg that are necessary for certain movements and corrections, though always maintaining contact with the horse. Further, the out-turned foot tends to make the rider grip with the calf of his leg, a form of contact that is more aggressive and less sensitive than the correct contact with the flat inside of the leg.

It is worthwhile sometimes to do floor exercises to loosen the hip joints so as to widen slightly the distance between the tops of the two thighs, thus making it easier for the lower legs to enclose the barrel of the horse with the toes kept more or less to the front. But, whatever the legs do, or in whatever position they may be put from time to time, nothing must be allowed to interfere with the continuous contact of the seatbones with the saddle. And, in that context, the angle of the thigh should not be forced downwards to an unnatural extent. On the other hand, it is most important that the knee should not be so high that it cannot be moved backwards in conjunction with the lower leg, if required.

The lumbar spine

When the general position we have described has been adopted, the rider will notice that it produces a slight and unforced concave bend in the lower part of the back. This is of the greatest value and importance, and it must be maintained, albeit in a supple and easy manner, at all times and at all paces. This supple and unforced forward flexion of the lumbar spine must not be confused with the rightly condemned 'hollow back'. The latter is an excessive and forced posture that takes the weight off the seatbones, placing it more on the crutch and the inner part of the thighs.

The posture we adopt will simply ensure that the lower part of the spine is correctly positioned with a natural forward curve, so that it can operate efficiently in its dual role of absorbing shock or bumps and of carrying the weight of the torso forward with each step; the latter enables the rider to follow and accompany the movement of his horse in the most literal sense. He will also then be able to retain permanent and easy contact between seatbones and saddle, undisturbed by the sometimes powerful movements of his mount. The mobility of the lumbar spine is essential for this. The posture of the pelvis is exactly the same as that of the child who is told to 'sit up properly' on a stool that has no back support.

When we have acquired the skill necessary to maintain the saddle contact under all circumstances, so that we and our horse can move with mutual ease and harmony, then and only then shall we be able to influence the horse without inconveniencing him. Then we shall have acquired a good seat. Then we shall feel at one with our mount. Then our performance will both feel and look elegant and comfortable, showing no signs of that bumping and jolting and head-nodding that is unsightly and so obviously tiring to both parties. In order to appreciate fully how much can be achieved by a still seat, where the rider is glued to the saddle, it is

Figure 2 *Bracing the back*

probably almost essential for the beginner to go somewhere such as Aachen, or a European or World championship meeting, where he can watch a dozen or so of the world's best dressage riders in action – in competition or on the practice ground. Then he will understand its worth, and will be stimulated to ride as well himself.

In striving to achieve the permanent habit of a good seat, the rider must concentrate on three things. First, he must perfect his sense of balance to the point where he is not at all disturbed by sudden or unexpected movements of the horse. He should be able to follow any such movement without recourse to gripping with the legs or tightening his hold on the reins. Second, he must be supple and able to relax in all parts of his body, even when taking quick or sharp action with one or more of his limbs. This requires a lot of practice, including, almost certainly, regular exercises on the bedroom floor. Few of us will achieve the necessary degree of supple relaxation if we only practise on the horse's back, even with lunge lessons, and increasing age makes the floor exercises more and more essential. They represent the simplest, quickest and cheapest way of doing the job. Third, he must develop the muscular strength and control to be able to moderate the suppleness in each and any part of the body – especially in the lumbar spine – as may be required by the circumstances of the moment. The control of the back muscles enables the rider to use the loins, like a steel spring of variable tension, to influence and modify the movement of the horse's back without disturbing rhythm or contact. It is perhaps the most valuable asset of a dressage rider.

The development of the seat along these lines should be given priority over all other aspects of riding. The matter can be summarized in two short phrases. No seat, no rider. Good seat, good horse. It is difficult, though not impossible, to make major improvements in the seat without recourse to lunge lessons. Every rider of ambition and humility should certainly make frequent opportunities to have lunge lessons from a knowledgeable lunge master, if that is at all possible. But a great deal can be done by the simple expedient of persistent self-criticism and self-discipline, based on intelligent self-analysis. With determination, any fault, however deeply rooted, can be successfully rectified within a month or so.

The hands

The rider's hands are his most dangerous assets. With them he may at any moment, often quite unintentionally, cause his horse acute discomfort or pain. With them he may easily and quickly ruin his horse.

To use the hands to the best advantage, they should always and at all times be held in a manner similar to that of the person who is about to shake hands with a very delicate old lady. They will be in total self-carriage; they will have the thumbs uppermost; the wrists will be straight; the finger muscles will be soft; and they will advance straight towards the point of contact, thus making it easy for the old lady to receive them. Then they will not hurt her. Then our hands will almost speak for us.

The point of contact for the rider's hands is the bit in the horse's mouth, at the end of the reins. There are few rules in horsemanship so important as the one that says that the hands should always be in a straight line between elbow and bit. There they are at their most sensitive, both to feel and to speak. There they will have maximum control with minimum force.

It should be appreciated that, provided the rider's arms are totally relaxed, as they should be, the horse will, in stretching his neck to take a contact with his bit, actually pull the rider's hands up into the required straight line. Conversely, if the hands remain significantly below that line, it can only be because the arms are tense and offering resistance, or because the horse is not going forward in the proper manner. Almost invariably it is the former failing that is the main cause of the latter.

It is totally mistaken to suppose that a low position of the hands will induce a horse to lower his head. With the hands set in such a position, near the withers, the horse is more likely to raise his head, since his natural tendency is either to act against force or to avoid it altogether – in the latter case by coming behind the bit. There are few things more certain to spoil a horse's paces and freedom of movement than hands held too low. When they are held too high, above the line, it is the lesser of two evils.

The use of spurs

Spurs are very much a double-edged weapon. For the good horseman, they are almost essential for the refined development of his skills; yet, for the poor rider, they can encourage or induce all sorts of bad habits, and can ultimately do more harm than good.

For the rider who has acquired a firm, still and independent seat, and whose legs can be relied on to remain precisely in the position appropriate to the action of the moment, spurs provide an additional aid of great subtlety, precision and effectiveness. They put an edge on the somewhat blunt leg aid; they can be used in several ways, varying from a touch or a gentle forward-stroking action to a sharp or even severe prod; and, being made of metal, they are felt more immediately by the horse and consequently tend to produce a more instant response than the soft leather of a boot that is backed only by large areas of relatively soft human muscle.

But, even when worn by the best riders, the spur should only be used very occasionally to accentuate or improve the normal leg aid. It should be regarded as a tactical reserve that should not be squandered. The whole effectiveness, both physical and psychological, of the spur is soon lost if the rider gets into the habit of using it continuously, instead of the leg, so that the horse becomes acclimatized to its feel as one of the things that he has to put up with, however sharp, hard or painful it may be. He will soon become sour or numb, and will come to ignore all other aids. Then he is three-parts ruined, caught in a vicious circle in which ever more and more spur appears to be the only answer.

The bad or poor rider, who cannot keep control of his legs or who tends to turn his toes out or down whenever he gives a leg aid, will frequently touch his horse with the spur when he does not intend to. That, of course, is both unfair and confusing to the horse, who will never be sure whether the spur aid was intended to mean something or not. The horse's reactions and responses will accordingly become increasingly erratic and unreliable, leading, in all probability, to increasingly irritated and illogical spurring from the rider, and to ultimate chaos. At the very least, the bad rider, finding that his inefficient leg and seat aids are not producing the results he expects, will try to cover his inadequacies by resorting to the constant use of an aid that his horse dare not altogether ignore; he will thereby obtain some sort of result and will thereafter be tempted to neglect the essential cure of his riding faults – and cure alone will produce long-term and beneficial results. His spurs will have impeded his progress.

Types of spur

It is important to select and use the type of spur most suited to the conformation and sensitivity of both horse and rider. One type or shape is not necessarily suitable for all occasions or all horses. Riders should therefore realize the advisability of having several pairs in their tack room to choose from, according to the horse they are going to ride and his state of training. The significant differences in design will relate mainly to the length and shape of the shank and to the existence (or not), and degree of sharpness, of a rowel.

The main factors that should govern the selection of the type of spur are as follows:

1   The shank should be of appropriate length and shape to permit the rider to touch his horse with the tip without having to make any major adjustment to the position of his leg, and with the least possible raising of the heel. A great deal will depend on the length of the rider's leg and the shape and size of the horse. In this connection, the shape of the shank should also be such that the rider will have no difficulty in ensuring that he does not touch the horse unintentionally. Spurs that turn inwards are usually unwise for this reason. On the other hand, spurs that turn downwards are less easy to use with lightness and precision because the tip can never be pointed directly towards the horse.

2   The sharpness of the spur may vary from the blunt end of the unadorned metal shank, to the relative sharpness provided by some sort of rowel. The plain or blunt type can be regarded as the basic or all-purpose spur, though some horses may tend to take insufficient notice of them. But, if poor riders have to wear spurs, they should, in fairness to the horse, always be blunt. For better riders, it is preferable to use spurs with rowels rather than continue to increase the prodding with the blunt type. Too strong a use of blunt spurs can easily bruise the horse.

3   Rowels themselves may be either in the form of a small coin with a smooth or slightly ridged circumference, or have varying degrees of pricks. The former merely serve to reduce the bluntness of the normal spur shank, while the latter will increasingly cause the horse to respond sharply to the touch, as the pricks tend to puncture the skin. For all normal purposes, there should never be any need to use rowels sharp enough to break the skin or cut the flesh, even when used as punishment. Spurs sold and purchased with sharp-pointed rowels may easily be filed down until they cause no pain when rolled across the palm of the hand.

The use of the whip

The whip is an absolutely indispensable training aid that should be carried at all times, notwithstanding the fact that it may not often be used. For the very young horse it forms the essential link between lunge aids and riding aids. Later, it will have very many uses, from acting as a reinforcement to a leg aid to almost doing the work of an additional leg. It can encourage a horse to work a little harder or it can speak severely, if not necessarily loudly, to bring an inattentive or recalcitrant horse to order.

Even more than the spur, the whip can be used with infinite variations of severity; at the least it gives a gentle whisper of encouragement. Only the sourest of horses will disobey or ignore the whip, however lightly it is used. On the other hand, a few horses, including those that have been badly treated at some stage, may resent its use and react by kicking against it or by throwing their heads up. In all such cases it is imperative that teaching the animal to accept the whip by kindly means should be given priority in the training programme. He must learn that it is not an enemy, but just a part of the language that he has to understand. But it would be very wrong and unwise to try to instil that lesson by flogging the horse into a forced obedience. An intelligent, patient and gentle approach will pay a far better and more lasting dividend. But, until the whip is accepted in a rational manner, it will be very hard to make serious progress.

Since the most fundamental use of the whip is to reinforce a leg aid that has not received adequate response, the rider must take care always to apply it immediately after a properly applied leg aid, and never before it or on its own. Similarly, it is important that the horse should be allowed the necessary freedom to respond to the whip in the appropriate way, and not be so tightly held in that no free response is possible. The use of the whip in such circumstances can have no intelligible meaning to the horse, who will inevitably come to regard it as incomprehensible and unfair treatment and so become resentful and nervous.

There are good whips and bad whips, and naturally a good rider should take care to provide himself with a good one. A good whip should have the following features: (a) it should be between 90 cm and 105 cm long (3 feet to 3 feet 6 inches) so that the tip can be made to touch the flank of the horse, behind the rider's leg, without any excessive movement of the hand, which would interfere with the bit. Whips of 115 cm or 125 cm (3 feet 10 inches or 4 feet 2 inches) in length are unnecessary for ordinary purposes, difficult to control and tend to look unsightly; (b) it should be light and well balanced, for ease of control, the point of balance coming about a quarter of the way down the shaft from the head, which should have a small knob to prevent it slipping through the hand. The handgrip should not be so thick as to interfere with the finger control of the reins; (c) it should be so constructed that a small action of the wrist will obtain a quick but controlled flip from the tip of the whip only, but without any

Figure 3 *Use of the whip*

appreciable counter movement or bellying effect in the middle of the shaft. If the whip responds by bellying in the middle, it will be as awkward and undesirable to use as a bad fishing rod.

There are many makes of whip on the market, most of them quite inexpensive, so it pays to shop around to find one that is going to be suitable and a pleasure to ride with. Those sold as polo whips are to be avoided as they are usually much too 'whippy'.

Failure to hold the dressage whip correctly can have a seriously harmful effect on the rider's hands. Correctly held, with the hands remaining in the proper riding position with the thumbs uppermost, it will lie close behind and nearly parallel to the rider's lower leg, resting lightly across his thigh. In that position it is ready instantly to act in support of the leg with the minimum distance to travel; it is kept steady against the thigh so that it will not flip about and perhaps touch the horse unintentionally; and it looks tidy and workmanlike.

If the whip is seen to be sticking out to the side, away from any contact with horse or rider, or if it is pointing back towards the horse's quarters or stifle, perhaps lying close underneath the rider's arm, it is a certain indication that the rider's hands are no longer in the correct position. Either the thumbs will have been turned inwards, thus making the whip stick out to the side; or else they will have been turned forwards and down, causing the whip to be more or less parallel to the ground. Both are bad hand faults as they cause wrists to become stiff. Thus the whip provides the rider with a means of keeping a check on his hands.

3

Preparations for the Horse

Minimum requirements

We must assume that the horse we have taken on into the higher education of advanced dressage will have shown himself to have qualities that are at least a trifle above average in the basic training covered in *The First Two Years*. We need not put it higher than that, though naturally the brighter he shone in that early work, the brighter his prospects will now appear, and the more exciting will be the secret dreams of his rider.

To be more precise, to make it worthwhile investing in a ticket for this new and probably lengthy journey, the horse should have developed a well-proportioned musculature sufficient to stand up to the considerable strains that he will have to face; he should have acquired a satisfactory and submissive degree of suppleness not least in the back, neck and poll, both lateral and longitudinal – the latter being particularly important since it implies an overall roundness that alone can enable the horse to engage his quarters to develop the collection and the lightness for advanced work; and he should be proficient in all the airs of the basic training, including simple lateral work in all three paces, and be competent and consistent in the simple flying changes of leg. None of these things need be perfect, but we must be confident that they can be performed and practised without stress or struggle and to a standard that is genuinely satisfactory or fairly good. In particular, we must squarely face the fact that it is no use getting involved in serious ambitions for advanced work if there is any form of persistent fight or resistance going on between the partners. In other words, calmness and willing co-operation must be the norm. And it goes without saying that the horse must be sound.

The extended trot

It is possible, and even likely, that some riders will, at this stage, be rather less than satisfied with their horses' extended trot, which they may feel merits a grading no higher than sufficient. If that is the case, the rider should not be deterred, but should take courage and press on. The extended trot is not at all a simple matter and can be expected to improve considerably as the horse's overall gymnastic performance is tuned up and developed. If the worst comes to the worst, it is possible to go a very long way and have a great deal of interest and fun without it, though that is not to suggest that it should be neglected. Certainly no training can be considered complete without a satisfactory degree of extension, but it is one of several movements, including the piaffe and the passage, in which by no means all horses are able to achieve a high or classic standard. In any case, there are different degrees of extension, so we can take comfort from the fact that a small extension is still an extension, provided that it is produced in correct form – even though it may be little more than some other horses would show as a medium. It is far more valuable to be able to show a good quality mild extension with steady rhythm and balance, than a forced or exaggerated big one. The problems of extensions are discussed in detail in Part Two (chapter 6).

The contact

At first, the strength of the contact with the bit may well be somewhat stronger than one would like, but that is not necessarily a matter of any serious concern, provided the horse retains a degree of elasticity in his back, neck and poll. The lightness will improve as he becomes stronger in his loins and learns to engage his quarters more effectively. It would be of much greater concern if the contact was too light, with the rider unable to increase it at will because the horse was hanging back.

The ideal contact, in which the rider can rely solely on the weight of the looped rein, can be achieved only much later on and then only by master horsemen. In any case, and at whatever stage of training and horse-manship, the true impulsion flowing through the supple, swinging back by which the horse constantly demonstrates his urge to go forward, must never be sacrificed for a spurious or artificial lightness. We need impulsion and straightness first, and lightness after that. A good, positive, and even strong contact is better by far than too little, and should certainly be expected and accepted without fear by the less experienced riders. Such a contact gives a pleasurable and exciting sensation of having power to play with; it increases the confidence of both parties in the other's performance; and it provides a basis for the attainment of the vitalizing longitudinal elasticity of the horse's back – provided there is no stiffening or resistance. With that proviso, the rider will be no more inconvenienced by a strong contact than will a yachtsman when the wind pressure in his sail increases from a gentle zephyr to a strong breeze. He will revel in its effect and in his increased ability to show off his boat.

The supple back

Longitudinal elasticity is an essential element in true impulsive collection, and will be discussed again in that context in the next chapter. Without a steady and sufficient contact with the bit, acting on the joint of the poll, the rider has no power to make the horse round his back and get his

a

Stretching the horse's spine (rising trot)
*Both pictures show the horse stretching his neck downwards and forward to extend
the natural curvature of the whole spinal column, thus releasing back-muscle
contraction.*

*Impulsion is maintained to keep the quarters well engaged with full track-up of the
hind feet. The swing of impulsion through the body is also apparent from the length of
the stride.*

*In (a) the rider has just asked for more left flexion, thereby temporarily reducing the
amount of stretch. However the shoulders remain free, as indicated by the elevation of
the forward moving right foreleg. The horse is not 'on the forehand', despite the low
head carriage. He carries himself with a light but steady contact, the lift in shoulders
being apparent.*

*For short periods of work the stretch can be even lower, with the nose down to at least
the level of the knee. The line of the face is, and should be, behind the vertical, maintaining the natural curvature of the spine and flexion of the poll (see page 52: Stretching)*

b

hindlegs further forward and underneath him. It is physically impossible for the horse to do this unless his back, and the muscles that control it, are strong enough to emulate, in a very small way, the action of a galloping greyhound, whose back is so supple that his hindlegs can swing right forward and past the forefeet. Without his wonderfully supple back, the dog could not begin to do this. The same principle applies also to the man who tries to ride a bicycle up a steep hill. If he sits bolt upright with a straight, stiff back he will never get up the hill without dismounting. If he lowers his head and rounds his back, he will immediately be able to develop the power of his loins and thighs to a far greater extent and will be able to ride up much steeper hills.

So it becomes clear that, whether it is the man on the bike, the greyhound or the horse, strong, supple and free back and loins are essential prerequisites for the full use of the hindlegs. To achieve that condition is a prime, recurrent and never-ending task for the advanced dressage rider.

On the bit

That the horse should be 'on the bit' in all his work should need no detailed elaboration. The FEI Rules for Dressage state that requirement in those very words. It is mentioned here only because so many British riders still appear, after more than thirty years of playing at dressage, to be unable to grasp the true meaning of the expression or appreciate its overriding importance. All sorts of excuses are offered to explain a failure to comply with the requirement. The horse is said to be too young; he has only been out of his stable for ten minutes and has not yet agreed to come on the bit – and many others. Needless to say, all such explanations are valueless, the simple and unequivocal fact being that once the horse has begun his work, no excuses are valid and only poor horsemanship can explain the failure. There is never any necessity or excuse for a human being to move around in a poor posture once he has left his bedroom in the morning. The same principle applies to the horse.

A horse can and should be expected, to a greater or lesser extent, to work on the bit from the day on which he is first backed and from the moment in his subsequent daily schooling when he has shaken the cobwebs out of his hair and has walked perhaps a couple of hundred yards from his stable door. He has been working in that way from the day when he first had the side reins correctly adjusted in the early stages of his education on the lunge. There is nothing unkind or painful about it. It puts no unnecessary or unacceptable pressure on his physique or on any part of his body. Being on the bit should be regarded quite simply but firmly as the horse's normal working habit and posture, the posture from which he is able to make the best use of himself. He is at attention. He is carrying himself, and he can control himself. He can be controlled.

It should be remembered that being effectively on the bit involves two things. First, the horse has to be put into the ramener, which means only that, as the result of minimal impulsion, the face line should be at or close to the vertical. Second, the horse has to be activated sufficiently by the use of appropriate seat and leg aids so that he begins to work positively forward and up to the ramener or, in other words, up to the bit. In that position, the rein tension, even if it is quite strong, will not interfere with the transmission of impulsion from the quarters, through the back, and into the forward-stretching neck. It must be the rider's aim to maintain that free flow of impulsion, which he will receive and feel in his hands in every step and every moment of the work, just as the yachtsman needs an absolutely constant feel of wind in his sail. If the impulsive feel begins to fail, he must take instantaneous action to refresh it. Indeed, to be successful, the rider must anticipate the failure by means of a highly tuned sensitivity and awareness of all parts of his horse. The speed with which a constantly recurring impulsion failure is corrected and revitalized is one of the main hallmarks of a good horseman. If he can succeed in that he will succeed in most things.

Recapitulation

No movement, however trivial, should be written off and forgotten once learnt. Each and every lesson has its own place and its own part to play in the horse's repertoire. There was a perfectly good purpose for its original introduction, perhaps in the very early stages of training, and its usefulness will continue to be significant throughout the long search for total harmony. In this way we build up an ever-enlarging vocabulary for our increasingly well-educated horse. Each phrase has to be perfected in his understanding, as well as in his purely physical ability, and it is through this blending of the physical and the mental that we progress towards the harmonious fluency of action that we dream about and which makes the well-trained and well-ridden horse such a pleasure to watch. But it takes time and progress cannot be hustled.

As we make that progress we shall find that the most complex and difficult movements are all based on relatively simple aspects of basic training, and that is why the latter must be practised and polished at least as often as the more complicated later developments. The concert pianist never ceases to practise his scales, and in the same way the rider must frequently, even daily, take his advanced horse back to refresh him in all the simple stretching, loosening and suppling exercises in addition to the basic movements such as leg yielding and shoulder-in. The more we ask of our horse, the more he will tend to become stiff, tense and not-forward, unless we take regular and frequent steps to counteract that tendency.

The snaffle bridle

During the last stages of *The First Two Years,* we began to use the double bridle quite often. But, now that we have decided to proceed into the sphere of advanced dressage, we must quite firmly put that double bridle away with our Sunday suit and revert to the plain snaffle for virtually all our schooling. From now on, we shall be trying constantly to take old movements a stage further towards perfection (which of course we shall never reach) and be struggling to master the first steps of some new and difficult problem. In either case, the snaffle is by far the best tool for the job. Conversely, the double bridle incorporates certain dangers, some of which are so subtle that we may not be aware of them until it is too late and damage has been done; the horse may be so inhibited in his work that he begins to exert mental or muscular resistance. There is no movement that cannot be taught more safely and more profitably, and then developed more quickly, in a snaffle than in a double. When the work can be executed in a snaffle without tension, argument, difficulty or loss of balance in horse or rider, then and only then should the double bridle be called for to help add the glitter and put the icing on the cake.

There are three interrelated aspects of all dressage training. First is the matter of the rider's understanding of exactly what he is trying to do and of his ability to control and co-ordinate his smallest bodily actions towards that end. He should, of course, also know why he is doing it. Second is the matter of the horse's understanding of what exactly he is being asked to do and of his physical fitness and ability to execute the task demanded. This will be shown by his quick and easy response to his rider's various aids. And third is the remarkably difficult matter of co-ordinating the resulting activities of the two parties as they struggle to overcome their respective incompetences. In the resulting turmoil it is inevitably the horse that tends to suffer most. It is therefore vital, for humanitarian as well as mechanical reasons, that the rider should have in his hand a tool that will cause least pain, harm, fear or inconvenience to the horse during those moments of incompetence that will assuredly occur. The plain and uncomplicated snaffle bit is just such a tool, and we shall use it for all positive teaching sessions, right up to the highest levels. To use the double in those circumstances can only complicate the problem and exacerbate the difficulties, besides being psychologically unsound.

The double bridle

The danger in the use of a double bridle for routine schooling is that, with so many other things to think about, the rider may, momentarily or for longer periods, unwittingly exert a greater pressure on the curb rein, and consequently on the lever of the bit, than he intended. But the horse will be acutely aware of it, becoming anxious, confused and possibly resentful of what will seem to him to be unreasonable interference and discomfort. In self-defence he will try to ease his discomfort either by stiffening his jaw or by ceasing to go forward into the bit. Either reaction will immediately spoil his work and is likely to become habitual.

The correct and effective use of a double bridle is a more intricate and complex matter than using a snaffle. It is much more than just putting two bits in the horse's mouth instead of one, with the hope that everything will be magically improved – as is all too frequently done. No rider should use a double for the first time until he has acquired a thorough knowledge of what it is meant to achieve, its mechanical processes, how to fit it, and how to use and operate it. And, being a comparatively complex tool, it requires relatively skilful handling by the rider. Similarly, no horse should be expected to work in a double bridle until he has received some hours of quiet introduction to its niceties and purposes. That introduction should initially take place in the stable, to be followed a day or so later by several short periods of quiet riding, first in walk and later in trot, on more or less straight lines, with only brief and occasional contact with the curb rein.

This introductory or instructional phase – much of it taking place at the halt or at the walk – is of great value in providing time for both parties to feel and to test their own and each other's reactions to the new piece of equipment under varying circumstances. The horse gains confidence that the new device in his mouth, despite its great and easily appreciated power, is not intended to hurt or bully him. But above all else, he will learn from the good rider that a ready submission will bring immediate release from its demands. The teaching of that lesson becomes the rider's first duty.

The rider, for his part, will be reminding himself that he now has two bits instead of one at his disposal; that they act in different ways and should be used accordingly; and that he must contrive never to grasp the reins in such a manner that the two bits act together on the bars of the horse's mouth in a crude amalgam of their respective powers. Failure in this respect will bring about the ruin of the horse's mouth and of the quality of his work.

The parts of the double

The bridoon, or snaffle, in a double bridle provides, as does the snaffle used by itself, the basic means of contact and control by the reins. It never varies significantly in its action, with the result that the horse comes quickly to accept its stability and simplicity, and is not afraid when he is asked for additional impulsion. It forms the permanent bond between horse and rider that should never be broken.

The curb bit has the sole function of reminding the horse, through its lever action, to keep his jaw relaxed and consequently sensitive to the light actions of the rider's hands and fingers. The mouthpiece of the bit achieves this end by its slightly downward pressure on the bars of the mouth as it pivots round the fulcrum of the curb chain. It is important to remember that the mere weight of the bit, together with that of the attached rein, will itself effect a gentle pressure all the time, even when the rider is exerting no tension with his fingers. The weight of the bit, gravity and the position in front of the vertical of the horse's head will see to that. Such pressure will be lighter than the lightest action of the hands, but to that extent the curb bit will be self-operating and should be given the chance to be so. Only if the horse becomes neglectful of the curb should the rider bring his finger influence into play to increase the bar pressure momentarily before reverting once more to the norm. The finger pressure on the curb should never be maintained indefinitely since that would create numbness and prolonged resistance in the horse's mouth.

The rider must always be aware of which combination of the two bits he is using at any given moment, and of the reason for his choice. But since, as we have already said, the bridoon is virtually always in action, his chief concern will be when and to what degree to use the curb in combination with the bridoon. The contact with the latter should not be lessened just because the former is brought into play. The rider's ability to act with discretion and precision in this way will depend very much on how he holds and separates the four reins.

Holding the reins

There are several ways in which the four reins of a double bridle can be held, though only two are commonly used. The three-in-one method in which both curb reins and the nearside bridoon rein are held in the left hand, and the off-side bridoon rein only in the right hand, is conventionally used in the Spanish Riding School but is seldom seen elsewhere. It makes separate use of the bridoon and curb reins, or of one curb rein independently of the other, extremely awkward, and raises problems regarding the position of the hands. The late Colonel Alois Podhajsky, commandant of the school for many years, once explained that this method merely made it easier for the rider to transfer the reins to one hand when removing his hat in salute.

By far the most common practice is to hold the reins in their normal pairs, with the bridoon rein in each pair on the outside of the fourth or little finger, where it will most conveniently do most of the work, and with the curb rein inside it, passing between the third and fourth fingers, the loose end of both reins passing out of the hand over the top of the first finger where they are held firm by the thumb (Figure 4). But this conventional method is hardly sufficient to make the separate use of the curb rein a very practical possibility. To achieve that end, it is helpful to have the loose end of the curb rein coming out of the hand between the first and second fingers, the loose end of the bridoon only coming out between the thumb and first finger. The first finger will separate the two loose ends. With the reins held in this manner, the thumb and forefinger maintain the normal grip on the bridoon to prevent it slipping through the hand, while the two middle fingers act together in complete freedom to increase or release the pressure on the curb. Minor adjustments to the pressure on the bridoon are made by the little finger.

If the loose end of the curb rein passes, with the bridoon rein, between thumb and forefinger, it cannot be totally released and its separate use will be severely restricted. It will also then be virtually impossible to adjust the respective lengths of the two reins while in motion. Held in the manner described in the previous paragraph, the two middle fingers can play the curb rein quite independently of the bridoon, and can even let it slip or lengthen for an inch or so on its own. In short, it provides the rider with the ability to use the curb with great delicacy and precision, and helps him

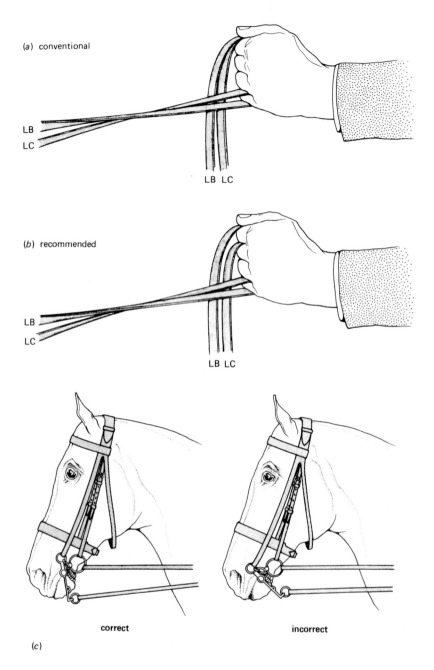

(a) conventional

LB
LC

LB LC

(b) recommended

LB
LC

LB LC

correct   incorrect

(c)

Figure 4 (a and b) *Holding double reins (LB – left bridoon, LC – left curb)*
(c) *Double bridle. Fitting the curb chain*

to keep less tension on the curb than on the bridoon. The latter point should always be noticeable. With this method he can be quite confident all the time that there is no unwanted tension on the curb for the simple reason that it is easy for the second and third fingers to remain relaxed while the thumb, forefinger and little finger grip the bridoon rein quite firmly.

The curb chain

Correct and efficient fitting of the curb chain is often neglected or misunderstood. A maximum angle of 45 degrees between the cheek of the bit and the bars of the mouth, when the bit is fully operated, is usually said to be satisfactory. There is, however, a danger that a fitting that looks all right in the stable will appear obviously too loose when under pressure of action by horse and rider – though of course the latter cannot then see what is happening. When this occurs, riders are often seen to be working with the cheeks of the curb bit pulling back perhaps to a 90-degree angle, almost parallel to the ground, in which position the correct action of the bit is destroyed. In this extreme case, the curb chain ceases to have any lever effect, the bit being pulled back against the bars of the mouth by direct action of the rein, working exactly like the bridoon except that the chain will be pinched against the corners of the lips. In a less extreme but still faulty fitting, the bit will no longer have its downward pressure, tending to pull upwards to force the mouth open and creating unwanted pressure through the headstall on the poll. The horse will be in some discomfort. Even a slight tendency for this to happen is, of course, highly undesirable. In short, it is an illusion to think that having a loose curb chain is being kind to the horse. In fact it will be more efficient and more comfortable if it is on the short side rather than loose.

There is, on the other hand, very little at risk if the chain is fitted a little on the short side, so that the bit does not, at least in the stable, pull back to more than about 25 degrees or even less. The only danger in this would arise if the rider was not proficient enough to handle his reins discreetly. If he leaves the curb bit very largely to its own devices, as outlined in the earlier paragraphs, all will be well and the horse will remain comfortable. To a very considerable extent, the curb bit will, if allowed, operate itself efficiently by its own weight and that of the reins.

As with the snaffle, the bar of the curb bit should be smooth and round, and as thick as is convenient for the size of the horse's mouth. Both bits should have the same measurement: the width of the mouth measured from the outside of the lips, plus half an inch.

Working a horse

To work a horse usefully and productively, it is necessary to make the horse work. The last word in that sentence carries the main emphasis, and it is one that young riders often fail to appreciate sufficiently. It is quite possible for a horse to be ridden round an arena or manège for an hour or more in walk, trot and canter, in various conventional patterns, but with little or no serious advantage to his education or physical development. On the other hand, the rider who understands how to make his horse work, in the sense that every muscle and joint is brought into energetic and interrelated play so that the horse operates as a single piece of machinery, can achieve a great deal and twenty or thirty minutes may suffice for the day's work.

It is a common occurrence to see some experienced or professional rider mount a horse that normally makes little impression under its amateur owner, yet almost at once the animal is transformed and appears to have unlimited potential. That metamorphosis is not achieved by any special trick, but solely by the rider's ability, basic knowledge, experience, skill and, above all, by his confidence and determination that he will cause the horse to work with all the power with which he is endowed by nature. In doing that, the whole horse is exercised, all the muscles become supple and eventually stronger, and the horse quickly gains in balance and output. There becomes less and less time for any form of resistance, with the result that the horse begins to submit his full attention as well as his whole body to his rider. When this occurs, the rider has, to use the classic phrase, *put his horse to the aids*. From that moment, everything is possible.

Putting the horse to the aids

Each day, and at all stages, before anything useful can be done, the horse must be put to the aids. He will assuredly never put himself to the aids, if only because he does not recognize the necessity, and it therefore becomes the rider's first daily task. It is a task that must take priority over the whole of the programme that the rider will have sketched out for himself for the daily session. It may take anything from three to fifteen minutes, or occasionally longer, depending on the temperament and stage of training of each individual horse. But, however brief the time, it should be done methodically. The usual sequence is that first the horse must be loosened and stretched longitudinally; then he is suppled and made obedient to the lateral aids; and finally, when supple and loose, he is taken up by half-halts and urged forward to the bit to engage his quarters.

The job will be done, and the horse will be ready for progressive work, when the rider feels that a simple bracing forward of his back and leg aids will produce an immediate surge of energy, passing unmistakably from the quarters to the bit, through a neck that will be distinctly felt to lengthen, with no resistance in the poll. The horse thus puts himself into the rider's hands, at his disposal.

Problems for the rider

To make a horse work in this manner requires a high and sustained degree of activity by the rider, who must be alert, sensitive, responsive and physically fit. He must above all be confident that his theoretical and practical horsemanship has been developed to an extent that will enable him to apply the appropriate remedies instantly and effectively to the ever-changing conditions under the saddle. He has to sense or feel the inadequacies which the horse may momentarily show; he has to know, almost subconsciously, what must be done to correct or improve that condition; and he must be able instantly, and before the fleeting opportunity is lost, to make the necessary adjustments to his hands, shoulders, pelvis and lower legs in order to achieve that improvement. Almost before he has dealt with that situation, he must begin the next process of feeling, assessing and correcting.

And so it will and must continue. The horse must never 'go to sleep' or relax into a cosy or complacent inactivity. He is there to work and it is only through work that he will make progress. The horseman's ideal ride, when the horse does all his work perfectly upon the first and slightest indication from the aids, will always be for tomorrow. But we must ride for the moment, and that means work, and quite hard work, for the rider as well as for the horse. We must remember that the latter possesses enormous power, but he has to be made to use it. The quality of every dressage rider is very largely assessed by his ability to display, for all to see, the power of his horse.

Nevertheless, dressage training is not all a matter of postponing till tomorrow what we would like to achieve today, or of continual disappointment. A little progress here and there will bring intense pleasure that will be communicated also to the horse. Both parties will suddenly sense that something is being performed without any of the worrying stress and strain that had previously dogged the effort. Both will be aware that an important step forward has been made. Both will remember it and recognize it as a strengthening of the bond between them and as the foundation for even greater achievements still to come. Work will in future be easier but, with wider horizons, even more challenging.

None of this can happen unless and until the rider has drilled himself to operate with a total consistency of aids and techniques. Day after day, month after month, the alphabet of communicative aids must be crystal clear in their intentions and anticipated results. Even quite slight failures in this respect can only disturb and muddle the horse, as well as gradually and rightly destroy the rider's confidence in his own leadership. He simply must not go on riding inconsequentially and erratically, knowing this to be the case. And it should be obvious that the clarity and consistency of the aids should be established correctly from the very beginning of the horse's education. This can only be done if the rider is confident that he knows exactly how every basic aid, or combination of aids, should be applied and precisely what result he should expect.

It must be the rider's prime task to remove the mote from his own eye before he proceeds any further with the difficult business of trying to correct his horse's faults. No rider should expect to be taken seriously if he claims that he has tried but failed to correct some major and persistent fault or weakness in his seat, position or aids. And no serious and able-bodied rider should display any such major fault. Once it has come to his notice, it should and can be cured, by concentrated self-discipline, within a few days or weeks. This is no more than would be expected from any child learning good manners.

Systematic Work

Beyond certain points of guidance, it is not possible to lay down exactly how each and every horse shall be worked-in for its main lesson or for a competition. No one programme will suit the temperamental and physical idiosyncrasies of all horses, or indeed of all riders. But the principles upon which the programmes are best planned will be similar and may be developed along the following lines, for horses entering the stage of advanced training. There can by many variations.

1   *Relaxing:* The horse is walked on a loose rein for up to five minutes, including the time taken to ride from the stable to the work place. This walk must be active and ground-covering. It allows the horse to come to terms with himself, the fresh air and the weight and feel of his rider and saddle, before any serious demands are made of him. (Maximum time: five minutes.)

2   *Attention and obedience:* The horse is worked with light but shortened rein contact in a comparatively collected and rather slow walk for three or four minutes. It is very important indeed that the horse should not be pushed or hurried in this work. He should be allowed to take his time, to find his own rhythm, and to move each limb in a quiet and thoughtful manner – as long as he moves forward calmly and steadily, avoiding any form of tension that might begin to upset the correct and rhythmic four-time sequence of the footfall. The dreaded danger of the horse beginning to amble or 'pace' is unlikely to arise if the tempo is kept slow enough.

This short phase in the walk will include plenty of simple lateral movements such as the turn on the forehand, leg yielding, shoulder-in, pirouettes and half-passes. The object is quietly to gain the horse's attention after the almost total freedom of phase 1: to let him establish his own balance and self-carriage in a slow pace; to re-establish the primary principle of obedience to the leg, all under the easiest possible conditions, in which there is the minimum likelihood of, or reason for, resistance; and to make use of the four-beat walk rhythm, in which each limb moves quietly and independently, to soften and supple all the vast mass of muscles in the body, making them loose and permeable so that the blood and the power runs through them.

It is easy to observe how much more difficult it is for a horse to walk slowly in a properly co-ordinated manner than it is for him to take longer, freer and perhaps faster strides. He can be seen to be concentrating more intently on what he is doing, and this helps to erase any stiffness and resistance that may exist after twenty-three hours of rest in the stable. It is the same for the human being who tries to walk accurately along a straight white line on the ground. The slower he goes, the more difficult it becomes to place his feet accurately and rhythmically, and the more he has to concentrate.

For this phase to be effective, it is essential that the horse be kept active and forward, unhurried, light in hand, but wholly on the bit. (Overall time: nine minutes.)

3   Stretching: Relaxed and attentive, the horse can now be worked at a faster gait, which may be either trot or canter or both, but without haste and for the purpose of longitudinally stretching the bone structure and muscles of the spine, including the neck. This task is of the utmost importance and should never be neglected. On its success will depend the interrelated factors of the rider's ability to sit in comfort on a soft and swinging back during subsequent exercises, and the physical ability of the horse to lower and engage his quarters for collection and for maximum impulsion. The key to this achievement lies, as in most aspects of dressage, in the horse's ability and willingness to release his back from all stiffness or harsh contraction, so that it will remain resilient and flexible despite all the stresses that will be placed upon it from above and from behind. The back is the vital link between all parts of the horse, and the rider must feel that he has control of it; that it is at his disposal; that it appears to come up to him rather than to contract or withdraw from him. For the back to be in this desirable state, it must first be stretched so as to loosen it and enable it the more easily to counteract its natural tendency, especially when under saddle, to become hollow. Only when stretched and suppled can it be worked upon and strengthened so that it will eventually be able to round upwards to the rider and make true collection possible.

The human athlete or gymnast will often stretch his back when preparing himself for the track by touching his toes. So the horse, to free his loins and thigh muscles, must be made to stretch his neck forwards and downwards. Equine anatomy is such that this exercise is only fully effective if the neck is lowered so that the nose is at least as low as his knees, in which position the line of the face should be somewhat behind the vertical so as not to disturb or inhibit the natural stretch and curve of the back-neck-head line. The horse thus remains effectively 'on the bit'. This daily exercise, done just for a few moments, ensures that the horse knows that he is allowed and expected to stretch himself fully at times; he will be confident that he can do so without pain in his back muscles, and will be able with pleasure and relief to counteract the effects of constant collection.

The exercise of stretching, whether in trot or canter, or even in walk, should be done on a light contact so that the horse deliberately takes the bit down when invited to do so. He should never just be given a loose rein and allowed to stretch or not as he wishes. The rider should not be satisfied unless he can work his horse in trot, on a full 20-metre circle, on either rein, in the fully stretched position – and he must be able to do this at will, at any time. Then he will know that his horse's back is still unspoilt and that he can, with normal discretion, continue to make major collective demands on it. Conversely, if he cannot put his horse down, close to the ground, it will be for one reason only, namely that the animal has become stiff in the back and is unable, or thinks that he is unable, to loosen or stretch himself. He is then in danger of becoming flat or even hollow, in which state he will never be able to collect himself. It is better to take no chances and to use the stretching exercise as a check for a minute or two virtually every day. It can also usefully be used in the middle or at the end of a session, as a reward for hard work.

The key to carrying out the exercise is to keep asking for little flexions with the inside rein, preferably on a large circle, while maintaining a light but continually 'offering' contact with the outside rein, and always keeping the horse moving in front of the leg. Never release the contact altogether with either rein, and increase it immediately the horse raises his head. It will be easier to achieve success at first in rising trot, which imposes the minimum pressure on the back. (Overall time: eleven minutes.)

NB Phases 2 and 3 may be interchanged in order of use.

4   Putting the horse to the aids: With the horse now calm, loose, attentive and stretched, it only remains to put him to the aids with a few minutes of truly active and impulsive work, varying between collected and medium paces, and aimed at ensuring that he is responsive and ready for anything, quick and light off the leg but submissive to half-halts. The horse should now feel powerful in the quarters, but supple in the back; active from behind, but light in the hand. A few transitions and some shoulder-ins will ensure that there is no incipient crookedness; perhaps three minutes of this work, giving an overall time of about fifteen minutes, and we shall be ready for work at maximum effort for the next half-hour or so. And in the main lesson the horse must also work with all his power and will, always urging himself forward to his rider's restraining hands. It is the rider's task and responsibility to see that he does this consistently, step after step. The rider must never take a rest and leave it to the horse. He must, with the tools of hands, legs and seat, be continuously striving for improvement and for the realization of his dreams of balance, rhythm, impulsion and length of stride: the four factors that are the essence of a good horse that has been put to the aids.

Part Two

4

Collection and Impulsion

The two qualities of collection and impulsion are the inseparable twins of dressage training and they form the basis of virtually everything we strive to do. They are inseparable because they are so closely related and interdependent. It is impossible to conceive of collection without the prerequisite of impulsion. And impulsion itself actually and continuously breeds collection. Logically, it would be more appropriate to reverse the order and refer to the twins as impulsion and collection since the former must be regarded as the more important of the two and the one that has to be born first. But in practice most of us will probably continue to pair them the other way round from habit, for the sake of euphony, and because collection more clearly represents our ultimate aim and is therefore given pride of place in our minds.

Definitions

It is important that the rider should have a clear and precise understanding of the meaning of all the words he uses, or hears used, during his work with a horse. Unless he has this understanding he will not know exactly what he is trying to do and will not be consistent in his efforts to do it. Defining the words used to describe abstract or intangible qualities is never easy, but each individual should try to do it for himself. He will benefit from the mental discipline required and will increase his understanding of his subject. But for the moment, and to ensure that the reader and the writer are thinking along the same lines, we will assume that collection is defined as a concentration of the horse's forces, achieved by the engagement of the quarters, the flexion of the joints of the hindlegs and slight shortening of the base line. Thus the power of the horse is marshalled (collected) and available for instant use. The consequence of collection is that the horse's weight, placed by nature more on the forehand than the quarters, becomes more evenly distributed and is ultimately carried more on the quarters than the forehand.

For the present purpose, impulsion may be defined as energy from the quarters received into and contained by the hands of the rider, who then controls and directs it by means of the reins. The feel of impulsion is like the feel of the wind in the hand of the kite flyer, or the feel of the yachtsman holding the sheet of the sail of a small boat. There will be the same smooth and delightful tugging sensation that suggests great but controllable power. But, if the wind is lost, the kite falls to the ground and the boat drifts helplessly. Without that wind-in-the-sail feeling, the rider is relatively helpless because he has no impulsion and the horse will be lacking the urge to engage his quarters actively.

Obtaining impulsion

Because the horse is not a thinking animal he cannot accurately anticipate his rider's requests and has little idea what is going to be asked of him next. He therefore cannot be relied upon to maintain his own impulsion indefinitely, like a machine, according to the setting of the accelerator or the electric control switch. Impulsion, in the context of dressage, requires a good deal of positive and fairly tiring activity for which the horse has no recognizable incentive. It follows that impulsion, once obtained, will always have a tendency to dwindle and deteriorate. It becomes the rider's business constantly to re-establish or reinforce it with almost every stride, and he does this with frequent but almost invisible signals from his seat and more especially his legs. It is better to rely primarily on the legs to transmit those tiny but positive signals because the action of the seat may all too easily become harsh, distasteful and even disturbing to the horse, although there is always some degree of co-operation between seat and leg. Certainly the legs are capable of more sensitive variations in this context than the seat, which has virtually all the rider's weight on it, and are therefore best suited to the task.

Obtaining collection

We have said that collection cannot be obtained without impulsion, and this may require some further explanation. The rider already working at

A correct collected trot, with shortened and elevated steps (not tracking-up) and well maintained impulsion. Gabrielle Grillo on Wilhelm Tell

this advanced level will not need to be reminded that useful collection, which is collection that retains its element of impulsion, must be obtained from the back to the front. The bringing of the hindlegs a little further under the body mass, a little closer to the front legs, will never occur if the horse is at rest or idling. In the horse's natural state, without a rider, collection will occur only if he is subject to some external stimulation such as fear or excitement. It requires a degree of energy and activity quite beyond normal. In ridden work, when fear and excitement are absent, the necessary stimulation and resulting activity must emanate from the rider.

First, the rider must urge the hindquarters and hindlegs to push forwards, and in doing so also to reach forwards, more energetically than the horse would otherwise think necessary. But energy itself, bearing in mind our definition of impulsion, does not necessarily produce what we want. Our definition stipulated that the energy from the quarters must be contained by the hands of the rider. In other words, the energy created in the quarters has to some extent to be restrained and stored up within the horse, and must not be allowed to dissipate itself into the air ahead. It is like the steam that creates pressure in the boiler of a steam engine. If the steam from the hot water were allowed to disappear straight up the chimney, there would be no power to drive the engine.

In equitation, energy that results only in speed, with no stored-up reserve, cannot be regarded as impulsion, however hard the horse is working or fast he is going. There has to be an element of restraint exerted through the reins in order to restrain the forehand from giving way to the full pressure from the quarters. This can only be achieved with harmony if the horse has previously been adequately suppled in the longitudinal plane. Then, and only then, can the excess pressure from the quarters be absorbed by the upward swing of the back and neck, allowing the quarters to be lowered more easily and providing the rider with a reserve of power, as from a steel spring, that is replenished with each successive stride, and which is at his disposal.

It will be seen from the preceding paragraph how vitally important it is to develop the longitudinal suppleness and strength of the horse's back and loins from the earliest stages of his training, and to treasure and refresh that suppleness as greater and greater demands are made. It will also now be clear why we cannot ever get useful collection without the impulsion that alone causes the engagement of the quarters and the shortening of the base. It should also be clear that we cannot hope to obtain more collection than the combined suppleness and strength of the back can absorb. If impulsion is created beyond that point, the horse is bound to resent it and resistances of one form or another will be set up. Our whole training programme is geared to obtaining more and more collection, yet we must never forget that the necessary strength and suppleness take a long time to develop in such a large animal and we shall have to act with great sensitivity and tact. We cannot risk pushing our horse beyond his ability to respond so that he will begin positively to resist with his back, to stiffen and to go too fast. We have to show him how to strengthen himself, but we cannot actually do it for him. We must guide and encourage him, over a long period, to do it for himself.

Resistance of any sort is the negation of suppleness, and we have already discovered that suppleness is the essence of collection. Any trace of resistance is therefore totally out of place in collected work and must be removed by suitable exercises as soon as it occurs. If necessary, the horse must be taken back to easier and less demanding work until all traces of it have been eradicated. Then, with great tact, the collected work can be introduced once more but stopped again if the resistance begins to reappear. It often helps if the troublesome exercise is well mixed, in very small doses, into a sequence of other and much simpler movements. In that way, the horse's mind is kept occupied and he can be slid into the awkward movements almost without his noticing it. He does not then anticipate trouble and remains calm. All through his training the horse must be taken back again and again, to be re-stretched and re-suppled. And so should the rider himself.

The problem of obtaining collection is no exception to the principle that no horse can be better than its rider. If, therefore, the horse is to be made supple and strong in his back, the rider must see to it that he also is strong and supple enough to maintain perfect control over his own movements. A rider who is in the least stiff or harsh in his own hips, loins or back will assuredly ruin the softness he has tried to create in his horse's back and so the battle for collection will be lost before it is begun. The rider with ambitions to take horses up to the higher peaks of education must, throughout his career and at every stage of his work with each new horse, maintain a constant check on his own fitness for the job, particularly in the suppleness and controlled resilience of his loins and back. It is entirely fallacious to assume that, having once acquired a fairly good seat, that quality of seat will remain the same for the rest of life, without maintenance. Age alone will take its inevitable toll soon enough, but so also will carelessness and complacency.

Seat and aids

The horse is not a machine that can be switched to a certain gear, a certain rate of action or a certain degree of effort with the expectation that he will remain that way until the switch is altered. He has a definite mind of his own, but he is unable to forecast his rider's intentions and requirements beyond the one stride that results from a specific aid. Collection, therefore, like impulsion, has to be asked for by a more or less continuous sequence of subtle but similar requests so that ideally the rider is, and remains, in perfect harmony with and in perfect control of every stride and every part of every stride. This obviously requires very precise, very clear, very harmonious and very sensitive aids. It is the goal for a lifetime of self-disciplined practice and study, and it is a goal that can only be reached by those who have won for themselves a quiet, effortless and harmonious seat on a horse.

The hindquarters

We have established that impulsion, in the form of wind-in-the-sails, is an essential prerequisite for collection. We may now usefully end this discussion of those two vital ingredients of dressage by reminding ourselves that impulsion involves the mobilization of the quarters, the word 'mobilization' being used in its fullest possible sense. First, we activate and then we gather together under our control the power of the quarters for our own use. The horse's quarters and hindlegs are somewhat awkwardly put together and attached to the body and they are not easy for the rider to mobilize. It is consequently often advisable to begin the activating process by the easiest method, which involves moving them sideways, first to one side and then to the other. This lateral activity will lead only indirectly to collection but the looseness and obedience that we shall thus obtain from the quarters will be of great help to us thereafter. All lateral exercises, especially the shoulder-in but not excluding those of the simplest variety, must be practised frequently, and always with the ultimate vision of improved forward collection in mind.

The half-halt

The bond between impulsion and collection is clearly expressed in the action of the half-halt. That basic and ideally almost imperceptible action embraces the essence of the two qualities we are discussing. Effectively executed, the half-halt engages, checks and frees the horse's forces. It confirms the connection between the inseparable twins of collection and impulsion.

Finally we must remember that the well-trained horse will have learnt to collect himself in response to the lightest indications from the rider's back, legs and hands. The horse that has to be collected more or less forcibly will always be heavy in hand.

5

The Shoulder-in

The shoulder-in is without question the most useful and productive of all the exercises and lessons in the training dictionary and it is basic to all advanced dressage. It produces lateral suppleness, and leads to longitudinal suppleness; it induces collection; it provides the rider with the ability to straighten his horse, and also to control him with finesse between the inside leg and the outside hand. The further up the educational ladder the horse is taken, the more indispensable becomes the perfection of the exercise of shoulder-in. It follows that the better the shoulder-in is performed in the earlier stages of training – that is to say with suppleness, impulsion and correct alignment – the easier it will be to reach the higher flights of the dressage syllabus. As François de la Guerinière said of the exercise he invented, it should be practised every time the horse is ridden, no matter how advanced he may be.

There are many degrees of shoulder-in, varying from the barely discernible, in which little more is asked of the horse than that he should submit himself to the demands and control of the outside rein and inside leg, forming a slight curve round the latter, through the basic shoulder-in performed on three tracks, to the full flowering of the movement when performed on four equal tracks by an exceptionally supple and well trained horse. Throughout the whole range, no matter what the variation or degree of bend involved, the same fundamental principles of quality and usefulness apply, the exercise being assessed by the extent to which the impulsion is maintained right through the horse into the rider's hands, and by the extent to which the horse's hips remain virtually at right angles to the track or direction of movement. It is the latter point that dictates the all-important action of the inside hindleg.

Impulsion

The shoulder-in confronts the rider, as does every other type of lateral movement, with the problem of keeping up impulsion which, of necessity, has to flow along with the alignment of the horse in order to reach the rider's hands, although that alignment may not conform with the overall direction of movement (see Figure 5). In this connection we may usefully ponder the theory of the French School that the creation and maintenance of impulsion should be the sole and exclusive responsibility of the rider's legs, leaving all

Figure 5 *Basic lateral movements*
Note the difference between the travers and the half-pass in the relationship of the
horse's alignment and the direction of movement. The two exercises are quite dissimilar

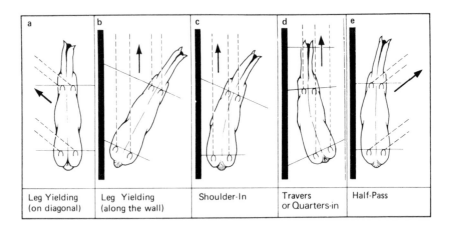

a	b	c	d	e
Leg Yielding (on diagonal)	Leg Yielding (along the wall)	Shoulder-In	Travers or Quarters-in	Half-Pass

‒ ‒ ‒ ‒ ‒ ‒ ‒ ‒ ‒ footsteps

————————— angle from track

arrow indicates direction of movement

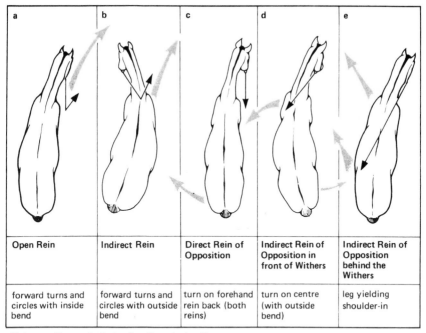

a	b	c	d	e
Open Rein	Indirect Rein	Direct Rein of Opposition	Indirect Rein of Opposition in front of Withers	Indirect Rein of Opposition behind the Withers
forward turns and circles with inside bend	forward turns and circles with outside bend	turn on forehand rein back (both reins)	turn on centre (with outside bend)	leg yielding shoulder-in

Note: small arrow indicates direction of rein effect
large arrow indicates direction of consequent movement of the horse

Figure 6 *Rein effects*

directional control of both ends of the horse to the hands and reins. This may be an ideal that is difficult to achieve, but it is by no means impossible, as a few moments' study of the five main rein effects will show (see Figure 6).

The horse's hips (See Figure 7)

In a correctly executed shoulder-in, the alignment of the horse's hips in relation to the direction of movement is of primary importance, since it directly affects the manner in which the hindlegs operate and their relationship with the animal's centre of gravity. When it is correctly performed, with the horse's hips remaining at right angles to the track but with the forehand brought in by the bend in the body, the inside hindleg will be moving forward and under the body and consequently directly towards the centre of gravity near the girth, thus inducing collection from that one leg and exercising its joints. But, if the hips are allowed to twist significantly towards the inside so as to reduce the need for the horse to bend so much, the inside hindleg would then, in order to keep on its track, have to move sideways and across, instead of forward and under, the body. And that makes all the difference (see Figure 7).

When the inside hindleg is allowed to move in the incorrect manner just explained, it will no longer be moving towards the centre of gravity; it will tend to remain more or less stiff instead of flexing in its joints, because the joints cannot bend in the sideways direction; impulsion will be reduced, and there will be no collecting effect. In short, the more the hips turn across the track, the more the useful effect of the shoulder-in will

Figure 7 *Shoulder-in*
(a) Correct shoulder-in
Horse on 3 tracks, inside hindleg moving forwards on track directly towards centre of gravity. Hip line square
(b) Incorrect shoulder-in
Quarters turned, horse on 4 tracks and with no bend; right hindleg passing across and under the horse but not towards centre of gravity, therefore not flexing. This is leg yielding
(c) Incorrect shoulder-in
Quarters turned, horse on 4 tracks with bend; inside hindleg not moving towards centre of gravity, therefore not flexing. This is leg yielding with a bend

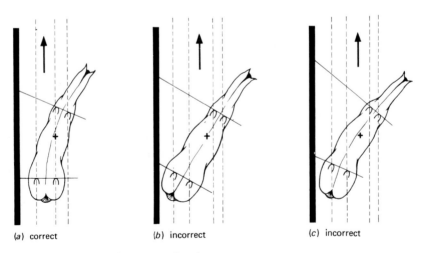

(a) correct   (b) incorrect   (c) incorrect

Note: + indicates approximate centre of gravity

be jeopardized. There is no escaping from this conclusion and the rider should study and understand the simple mechanics of what the horse has to do.

To underline just one point, we will take the action of the hock joint. The hock can only flex in one direction, namely the direction in which the horse's foot is pointing. Exactly the same principle applies to the rider's own knee, disregarding the fact that the knee points forward and the hock backwards. The direction in which the hock points, and is able to bend, is controlled almost entirely by the position of the hips, as is the human knee. If the hips are turned, the hock and the knee change their alignment and their direction of bend.

We know that, in the shoulder-in, the hind feet are expected to continue to move along their original track on, shall we say, the long side of the arena. But, if the hips are turned inwards and face diagonally away from the track, the hindleg joints can only bend if they actually move diagonally away from the track. But, in order to continue to move along the track as required, the hindlegs will have to swing sideways like stiff pendulums, because the hock joint will not bend that way. When that happens, the movement becomes nothing more than a form of leg yielding, a movement which is far less beneficial and important than the shoulder-in. These are vital matters, and we need make no apologies for considering them in depth.

Aids

If we assume that the horse is working smoothly, obediently and without resistance, the aids for the shoulder-in will be as follows.

Leg aids

The inside leg, from the seatbone down, acts well forward to create and maintain a lateral bend just behind the shoulders, supported by the outside leg acting passively behind the girth to prevent the quarters from falling out or twisting. Both legs act together, as necessary, to maintain impulsion. The inside leg pushes the forehand towards the opposite side, along an alignment parallel to the track on which the hindlegs are moving. It is extremely important that the lower part of the inside leg should stay well forward on the girth where it will not in any way affect the position of the quarters.

a

The shoulder-in
Both pictures show a correct basic shoulder-in, executed on three tracks, with impulsion forward into the rider's hands. In both, the inside hind foot is on the same line as the outside forefoot.

In (a) the outside hind foot is coming to the ground alongside the outside forefoot, indicating a full length of stride.

In (b) the inside hind foot (white coronet) strikes the ground alongside the hoofmark of the lifted inside forefoot, showing full engagement under the centre of gravity.

In both pictures the quarters remain virtually square to the track, thus making possible the long and engaged stride of the hindlegs.

In both pictures, the forehand is clearly turned inwards towards the centre of the

b

manège so that, in order to remain on the inner track, the inside foreleg has to cross in front of the outside one, thus suppling and stretching the shoulder muscles. See especially photograph (a)

Photograph (b) shows clearly how the hind feet continue to point and move straight along the track, facilitating the bending of the joints, while the forefeet, in conformity with the alignment of the shoulders, point diagonally across the manège.

In (a) the rider's inside leg has been pulled back a little and risks pushing the quarters out, although that has not in fact happened. The rider also looks down and allows his shoulders to become round. In (b) the rider's inside leg is placed, correctly, well forward on the girth

Seat aids

The inside seatbone is slightly weighted so as to encourage the inside bend. The body remains upright with the hips parallel to the horse's hips and free to swing with the horse in the direction of movement. The shoulders must turn inwards a little so as to remain parallel with the horse's shoulders.

Rein aids

The inside hand asks for and maintains the inside flexion and, with a very slight opposing tension in the direction of the rider's outside hip (the fifth-rein effect), complements the action of the inside leg (lateral aids) in encouraging the horse to move diagonally to the outside. The outside rein supports and controls the bend and the direction of movement, checking any tendency of the horse to move away from the track into a circle. Both hands receive the impulsion and are positioned slightly to the inside in order to conform with the bend.

In practice, young horses will seldom work with such a perfect blend of smoothness, obedience and lack of resistance that the textbook aids will be as easy to operate as they sound. Many little problems will almost invariably creep in, forcing the rider to make appropriate adjustments to his aids, though always trying to get back to the simple principal forms.

Examples of the use of shoulder-in

The importance of some degree of proficiency at the shoulder-in as an aid to the perfection of other movements will be seen from the following examples of its many uses.

1   *Preparation for the half-pass, in any pace*

The position of the horse in the shoulder-in is almost, if not wholly, ideal for the commencement of a half-pass. When performing, for instance, a right shoulder-in, the horse will be submitting obediently to the control of the rider's inside leg, which is essential also in a right half-pass. He will be bent to the right, while submitting to the control of his quarters by the rider's left leg. The shoulder-in position is only less than ideal in so far as the bend required in a good shoulder-in is slightly greater than that required in a half-pass. The distinction poses no serious problem because, when the moment comes to move from the right shoulder-in into the right half-pass, which involves an increase in the action of the left leg and a decrease in the action of the right or inside leg, the rider will almost instinctively and quite easily decrease the amount of bend. He will do this by opening the inside rein and acting more positively in an indirect manner against the neck with the outside rein (fifth-rein effect). In doing this, his outside shoulder will come back a little towards the normal position, and he will begin to allow his pelvis, which supports his torso, to swing to the right into the right half-pass. There will be more weight on the left seatbone and less on the right.

2   Correction of a bad half-pass

If a half-pass begins to fail, through diminishing impulsion, loss of bend or resistance, it is almost always undesirable to continue with the movement in the hope that it can be put to rights again. It is far better to break out of it and do something else until the faults have been forgotten and the horse is once again mentally and physically submissive to the idea of the half-pass. In those circumstances, one of the best and most obvious things to do is to revert to the shoulder-in, to re-establish confidence, before re-starting the half-pass. The rider only has to push his horse straight forward, out of the diagonal alignment into a shoulder-in position, by simply reversing the aids that took him into the half-pass in the first place. This excellent exercise can be repeated again and again, without any major change or disturbance to the horse's or the rider's position and posture – a few steps of half-pass right, followed immediately by a few steps of shoulder-in right along the original alignment, followed immediately by a few more steps of half-pass right, etc. This exercise not only helps to overcome the difficulties that arise in half-passes, it also greatly increases the mutual understanding and confidence between horse and rider. It also forces the rider to check on his ability to use his aids separately and discriminately.

3   Correcting crookedness

All horses have a strong tendency to be crooked – that is to say to move with their hindlegs not following precisely in the track of their forelegs – and it is virtually impossible, especially in the canter in which the tendency is strongest, to correct or counteract it by trying to push the quarters back into line with leg aids. Such a procedure usually ends with the horse drifting to the side, away from the original track. In the canter, when crookedness will invariably occur on the same side as the leading leg, a correction by the rider's inside leg, pushing the quarters back into line, will probably cause the horse to perform a flying change of lead which is certainly not required and will probably be disunited.

The only certain way of correcting crookedness is to cause the horse to place his forehand in front of his quarters, and then to hold it there while continuing the movement. To cure the habit, it will be necessary as an exercise to take the forehand even further to the side to which the horse is crooked, in the same way as one straightens a warped stick by over-bending it the opposite way to the warp. In short, if the canter is crooked, we deal with it by riding a shoulder-in to that side. When the canter shoulder-in can be performed with ease and consistency, it will be relatively easy to ride the horse in a straight canter.

4   *Ensuring straightness in the canter-depart, especially from the walk or the rein-back*

A horse has to make a special effort to push himself off into a canter from the slow pace of walk, and even more so from the static position of the halt. Since there is some movement in the rein-back, and probably also a more positive degree of impulsion, the transition from the rein-back to canter is slightly less strenuous for him than it is from the halt. But, in any case, the slower the initial pace, the greater is the tendency for the horse to escape the muscular strain on his loins inherent in any canter-depart by moving his quarters to the inside. He makes himself crooked.

It requires a considerable feat of horsemanship to overcome the problem of the crooked canter-depart or strike-off. To begin with, the rider has to overcome his own quite understandable tendency actually to force the horse to go crooked, if only to ensure a correct lead. In order to produce a depart from the halt into, for example, a canter left, he will probably push his left leg firmly into the horse near the girth in his effort to create the necessary impulsion. But in doing so he will also be pushing the horse's forehand slightly to the right, which is just where he does not want it to go. And, because he wants to canter left, he will in all probability have drawn back his right leg well behind its normal position on the girth. In that backward position his right leg, in trying to help create impulsion for the canter, will tend to push the quarters away to the left, thus positively creating the crookedness that he wants to avoid.

So what must the rider do? The answer is, at least in theory, quite simple, and lies in the word 'shoulder-in'. In the preceding walk, halt or rein-back, the horse will, correctly, have been perfectly straight. But, in the very moment of the strike-off, as he lifts himself off the ground on to his outside or right hindleg for the initial phase of the canter left, he has to be ridden into a very slight shoulder-in-left which will be felt and seen as each of the other three legs comes to the ground in their turn. If the strike-off from the slow pace is an immediate response to the application of the aids, and if the horse then steps directly but ever so slightly into the shoulder-in position, there is no possibility of crookedness and the battle has been won. But in creating the shoulder-in effect, care must be taken not to cause or allow an excessive bend in the neck.

This answer to the problem is easy to understand, but considerably less easy to perform. The battle must be won, to misquote the Duke of Wellington, not so much on the battlefield itself as on the early training grounds where suppleness, straightforward impulsion and obedience to simple aids were taught. If those qualities have been well taught in the early stages, they will provide us with an infallible answer, in the form of a shoulder-in, to the problem of a straight canter-depart.

5   Entering and leaving the canter pirouette

This very important aspect of the shoulder-in is dealt with fully in chapter 10 (page 112).

Quarters-in (travers)

Complementary to the shoulder-in is the movement of quarters-in, better, if less logically, known as the travers (see Figure 5, page 64). In general importance and usefulness, the travers, like its counterpart the renvers, is not to be compared with the shoulder-in. It is far easier for the rider and for the horse to perform, but it does nothing for collection, impulsion or straightness, and indeed, if not used with discretion, can tend to incite crookedness.

The benefits derived from travers are mainly concerned with loosening and suppling the quarters and hip joints and, because it is always easier to move the quarters than the forehand, with improving the horse's ability to bend round the rider's inside leg. But, because the quarters are turned at an angle to the line of progression, the movement cannot induce increased flexion of the hocks, for the reasons that have already been explained at length on pages 65–6. For the same reason it is difficult to maintain, or even to create, impulsion in travers, and this is accentuated by the fact that the quarters are neither moving nor working through the line of the spine to the bit and to the rider's hand.

The movement does, however, assist in maintaining and improving freedom and rhythm in lateral work, because the horse continues to move precisely in the direction in which he is looking and into which the bend is leading him. This is a valuable psychological aspect of travers and renvers.

The alignment, or angle, of the horse in travers should conform precisely to the obverse of the rules for shoulder-in. That is to say, it should be ridden basically on three tracks, the horse bent evenly through poll and forehand, the head (instead of the quarters) facing straight forward along the track. But unlike the quarters in the shoulder-in, the shoulders in travers will not be exactly at right angles to the track because, whereas the former are positioned at the extremity of the spine, the shoulders are located some way back from the front end, along the bend. In the travers it is the line across the ears that should be at right angles to the track.

Renvers

Every aspect of the travers applies equally to the renvers. The only difference between them is that the renvers, because there is no wall or barrier to enclose the forehand, and no track for the horse to follow with his eyes, is the more difficult for the rider to control accurately.

In the travers, the forehand follows the track, the hindquarters being brought in and the horse moving on three tracks. In the renvers, the forehand moves parallel to the original track, the quarters remaining on it and the horse still moving on three tracks.

6

Extensions

The essence of a good extension is that the stride should become longer without loss of impulsion or change of tempo. It goes without saying that there should also be no loss of suppleness or rhythm. It follows that, given the two former conditions, the arc travelled by each foot will be flatter, or closer to the ground, than in a more collected trot. In practice, the whole horse will become a little longer from nose to tail and will become a little more ventre-à-terre as the supporting legs are stretched more to the front and to the rear at the beginning and end of each stride.

It is tempting for the less experienced rider to think that adequate extensions are relatively easy to obtain, but this is certainly not the case and grave risks are run by those who try to start this work too soon and with insufficient preparation. Each step in a properly executed extension makes far greater demands on the entire musculature of the horse than occurs in the more ordinary working or collected paces, and the greatest exertion and strain of all must fall on the loins, the weakest part of the body. The reason for this is clear enough if we remember how relatively easy it is for a human being to lift a heavy weight sufficiently to move it forward a few inches at a time, and how much greater strength is required, particularly in the back and loins, to lift the same weight forward a foot or more with each lift. Exactly the same principle applies to the horse when he tries to lift his own weight plus that of the rider in such a way that there is a prolonged period of suspension in the trot or the canter with an extension of the amount of ground the feet have to cover. It is even harder for the horse than for the human being, because the former cannot position his haunches and loins in as effective a manner as the human biped – close to the centre of gravity of the weight to be lifted.

Free, easy, round and light in hand in extended trot, but engagement of the hindlegs not quite balancing the action of the front. Rider at ease and perfectly unconstrained. Karin Schluter on Liostro

The quadruped cannot lift very much with his front legs, so has to do all the work with his loins, which are put under the same sort of strain as is the wrist and forearm of a man trying to lift a loaded shovel off the ground with only one hand.

To produce a true extension with fluency and grace, the horse must first have developed adequate strength in his loins so that he is actually capable of doing this work, and he must be moving with an actively swinging back and a built-up impulsion that is available for release. If the rider can produce these conditions, he will not find it too difficult to obtain a degree of extension, simply allowing the horse to lengthen himself by a very slight release of the hands, and by maintaining the impulsion and the swing by the controlling influence of his own braced and spring-like back. In brief, the rider sits a little closer and firmer, with lengthened and clasping legs, asking the horse to become a little more ventre-à-terre.

An extended trot of the highest quality. Both horse and rider appear effortless and remain in classic balance and posture. Only the rider's hands have moved forward to allow the horse complete freedom in his neck to conform to the greater length of stride. He remains lightly on the bit but unconstrained, despite the major effort being made.

The hindlegs generate the extra impulsion and operate in obvious harmony with the forehand.

The rider's lower leg remains still and on the girth, giving the horse confidence and urging him forward with invisible messages.

Calmness and relaxation is expressed in the carriage of the tail and amiable outlook. Ruth Klimke on Privatier

If the rider finds it necessary to stir up his horse by leg and seat aids that are cruder and more violent than those described, then he has not adequately prepared his horse in either the long or the short term, and he will get a result that is without grace, fluency or suppleness. In his effort to respond, the horse will tense and stiffen his back and loins, he will probably come above the bit, and his paces will appear forced. He will also become uncomfortable to sit on, making the rider appear inelegant and incompetent. The gulf between the previous work and the extension asked for has been too great for the horse to bridge in a controlled manner.

An extended trot in full suspension, obviously originating from collection but covering a lot of ground with big over-track and a high degree of engagement. Cynthia Neale on Equus

An active and impulsive medium trot showing a generous lengthening of stride and neck, but clearly not in maximum extension. The horse remains round in the back and neck and therefore also in the action of the front legs. Rider's leg well placed on the girth. Christine Stuckelberger on Granat

To be of any real value, an extension must palpably be a pleasure to both horse and rider. The horse must be, and must be felt to be, free, loose, balanced and unconstrained, with no stiffening in any part of his body. The rider must feel, and must be seen to feel, perfectly comfortable and at ease, and also in total control of each and every stride. If the rider is uncomfortable, he will inevitably make his horse uncomfortable and that in turn will destroy the freedom and swing of the back and consequently the rhythm of the whole performance.

For the horse, the most important points are that he should become a little longer and a little lower in the neck, while remaining lightly on the bit, thus allowing the back the extra freedom and swing that is needed for the transmission of the greater energy coming from the quarters. If the head and neck come higher, or the back begins to hollow or stiffen, it means that the rider is either sitting too heavily or is asking too much in relation to the degree of gymnastic ability available; or that he has prepared his horse inadequately and does not have enough impulsion; or he is sitting badly.

For the rider, the main points to watch are: he should not allow the small of his back to collapse, as this puts him behind the movement and creates unwanted pressure on the horse's loins; he should sit still, with perfect balance, and follow the movement of the horse forward with his seat and pelvis; his legs should lengthen rather than shorten, and they should continuously and consistently clasp and encourage the horse to exert himself by forward urges – never with disturbing backward kicks or prods with the spurs; and his hands should not drop below the straight line from elbow to bit – the wrists remaining loose, so as to receive but not restrict the flow of impulsion. In short, the rider must not allow his position to deteriorate in any way below that which he adopts in the more collected and sedate paces.

So far, we have used only the generalized term 'extension', but there are many degrees of extension to be considered and practised. It is obviously unwise for a trainer even to attempt the more difficult exercises before the lesser aspects of any movement have been mastered, and that rule applies at least as much to extensions as to anything else. A lot of harm can be done to a horse's confidence if too much strain is imposed on him too soon, and confidence plays a major part in this work. A horse should, quite early in his training, begin gradually to develop his ability to move in a medium trot for quite long periods or distances, but the degree of extension in the medium must be kept within moderate bounds and should not involve tight corners. Thus his muscles and balance will be built up until, one day, a full-blown extension will come fairly easily and certainly without any violent effort or disturbance. In any event, it is always unreasonable to ask for full extension for prolonged distances, and it is advisable to use the rising trot for the great majority of the trot extensions so as to avoid the risk of overstressing the back.

Such are some of the main problems to be overcome in extended work, and to which we can add a final word for the inexperienced rider with a young or green horse. He must understand and accept that it is at best useless, and at worst positively harmful, to expect to obtain extensions by merely urging the horse to go faster. Rather, he must approach the problem with the idea of gradually developing the extension through a steady improvement in the gymnastic quality of the collected or working gait.

7

The Rein-back and the Schaukel

The rein-back

Every horse is able to walk backwards without excessive strain, provided he is not hurried or forced. This is not an unnatural movement, though it is not very often made by a horse with no rider. However it is quite certainly more awkward for the horse to go backwards than for him to go forwards, and the movement must therefore always be treated with some delicacy. The physical problem for the horse is demonstrated by the fact that he is forced to adopt for it a gait that is entirely different from anything he uses for other movements. He moves backwards in two-time, in more or less accurately synchronized diagonal steps which provide him with the security of having two feet on the ground at all times, one on each side. This gait is quite unlike a forward walk and should not be confused with that of the trot because, in the rein-back, there is no question of any moment of total suspension. It is a careful backward plod, causing the minimum risk of disturbance to balance.

The awkwardness of the rein-back is explained by the basic biological and evolutionary fact that the hindquarters are designed for the prime purpose of propelling the horse forward and at speed, and their conformation is excellently suited to that job. But in the rein-back the quarters have to pull rather than push or propel, and for this they are ill-adapted because of the construction of the joints and more particularly of the hocks. The forehand has little propelling power in any direction, and the construction of the joints of the forelimbs renders them especially unhelpful during any movement to the rear. So all the work has to be done by the quarters, despite their conformational inadequacies.

It is not impossible for a horse to move backwards in the semblance of a trot or a canter, but those movements pose such difficuties and problems

Excellent balance and collection in the halt. The head could be a few degrees nearer to the vertical and show a shade more impulsion. From this position the horse is able to make a correct rein-back, the diagonal front and hindlegs beginning in unison. Rider's leg has gone rather too far back behind the girth, making it difficult to obtain immediate forward action. Jennie Loriston-Clarke and Dutch Courage

both to the horse and to the trainer that they have no place in the sort of dressage curriculum that we are considering in this book.

Practised with discretion, without force of any kind, and under proper control as regards straightness, speed and length of stride, the rein-back is a fine exercise for the horse's loins and consequently for his ability to collect himself. It is also a good mental training that tends to steady a horse that is apt to rush forward too ardently. It can be used repeatedly, and occasionally for quite prolonged distances, provided that the action is always calm and unhurried and that the horse is never pulled back by the reins. Naturally, and as with every other exercise, frequency and duration should only be increased in accordance with the horse's fitness, and we must never forget that the rein-back does make quite severe demands on the hocks and loins.

The rein-back should not be introduced as an exercise until the rider is confident of being able to obtain an immediate and generous forward response to light leg aids, with the horse stepping well into the bit without resistance in his back or shortening in the neck. This should be practised from the halt into the walk and also directly into the trot. When the rider is satisfied with these simple preparatory exercises, the rein-back can safely be asked for in the following manner.

The horse should first be put to the aids at the halt, and then asked to perform the halt-to-walk movement, for two or three steps only, two or three times, in order to alert him and to check that all systems are working. If all is well, we can ask for the rein-back next time, in place of the forward walk. To do this we apply *exactly* the same light but firm forward aids and, at the very moment that we feel the initial forward response and just as the first front foot leaves the ground, we firmly close both hands on the reins to prohibit further forward movement, despite the important fact that the legs continue to create impulsion for a moment longer, and indeed until the horse actually begins to step back. It is essential to wait for the initial forward response before closing the hands. Then the horse will happily convert his own impulsion into a backward movement of his own accord.

On no account must we try to pull the horse back with a backward tension on the reins; to ensure that this does not happen, it is advisable for the less experienced rider to wedge his elbows into his body, just in front of his hipbones, so that the upper arms are incapable of making any backward movement. For the same reason, the rider should not lean back as that, besides tending to exert a pull, will overload the horse's loins – the region that has such an important part to play.

When the horse finds that his forward impulsion is barred by the closed and fixed hands, he will quickly look for release and will find it in the opposite direction. He will step back. Immediately we feel the horse begin to move to the rear we must respond by partially releasing the pressure of the legs, though they must remain in position and contact on the girth ready to reapply impulsion if the horse begins to hesitate or, conversely, if he begins to go back too fast. A further variation of the same aids will cause the horse to halt when the required number of steps have been completed. It is important to note that hesitation in the backward movement is the signal for more impulsion, not for more pulling.

One, or at most two, steps will be sufficient response to begin with, and should immediately be followed by a pat and a vocal expression of approval. We should continue in this way until, probably quite soon, we are sure that the horse has understood and accepts the reaction that we require of him without argument or resistance, calmly and confidently. There will then be no difficulty in gradually increasing the number of rearward steps to a maximum of about six. Eventually we may want, as we have already suggested, to use the rein-back exercise very occasionally, and always calmly, for the width or even the whole length of the arena, though such an exercise should never be undertaken under circumstances of anger or irritation and its purpose should be very carefully considered.

With very young horses it may be helpful if the rider takes just a little of his weight off the seatbones by leaning very slightly forward while the horse is stepping back, but later on no movement of the body, the arms or the legs should be visible. Some riders will advocate positioning their legs well to the rear of their normal position, but this is illogical if we accept the principle that the rein-back is or should be the result of forward impulsion. In that case there can only be one place for the legs – on the girth.

If the horse tries to avoid the restraining effect of the reins by going over or above the bit or, as we have already mentioned, the backward steps become precipitate, the movement should be stopped promptly and the horse put back to the aids with re-established impulsion. A degree of impulsion must indeed always be maintained, the horse remaining in front of the rider's legs throughout the whole movement – that is perhaps the most difficult part of the exercise. If he is not in front of the legs (is not on-the-aids), the rider will have no ability to prevent him going back too fast, in fact out of control, if the horse so wishes.

The schaukel

The German word '*Schaukel*' denotes the movement in which the rein-back is followed directly by, and then alternates with, a forward walk, with no actual halt at either change of direction. The rein-back portion of the exercise is usually performed at least twice. '*Schaukel*' translates into

English as 'see-saw', implying the alternating action of a saw. In competition dressage, the number of steps backwards or forwards is always precisely stipulated, and very accurate execution is expected. It is, however, questionable whether the official rules have been sufficiently thought out in connection with the manner in which the steps of the forward movements should be counted. Being in four-time, that counting is considerably more complicated than the two-time rein-back.

A schaukel usually begins with a rein-back, for which the aids have already been discussed. For the change into the forward walk, the fingers cease restraining and begin to release, while the seat and legs simultaneously demand more positive impulsion. Thus the see-saw movement is achieved and repeated by first creating and then 'playing' the impulsion between the hands and the seat/leg aids, and can be continued indefinitely.

When well executed, the foot that moves, for instance to the rear, for the last prescribed step, should not become fully weighted as it touches the ground, and should be the first to move again in the opposite direction. In that way the smooth continuity and unbroken flow of a good schaukel is maintained.

8

Counter-Changes-of-Hand

Whatever the original meaning of the words chosen for this movement, a counter-change-of-hand means, in the dressage vocabulary, a direct change from a lateral movement in one direction to an exactly similar movement in the opposite direction. The horse follows a zigzag course and the actual counter-change takes place at the point, or points, of the zigzag where the change of direction occurs. In competitions, the movement virtually always implies a series of three or more half-passes.

In theory, once a rider can ride his horse correctly in a half-pass to the right or to the left, he can automatically ride a correct counter-change-of-hand. But in practice it is by no means as simple as that. Individual half-passes are one thing, but it is quite another to fit them together into one composite movement consisting of a whole series of alternating half-passes that flow, one into the next, with unbroken rhythm. The main problems, which all occur more or less at once, at the moment of the change of direction, are: the maintenance of impulsion; the change of the dominant aids; and the change of the horse's bend, flexion, direction and alignment. This combination of related actions requires a high degree of subtle feeling and timing by the rider. The horse's balance and rhythm will be the first things to suffer if the timing and accuracy of the rider's aids are faulty or if the horse's response to them is sluggish, resistant or anticipatory.

The difficulties confronting the horse are formidable, and cannot be overcome in a flash or all at once. The horse needs time, and he needs sensitive, clear and informed guidance from the rider to overcome the problems. He has been bent and flexed in one direction, and he must then quickly bend and flex in the other; one lateral pair of legs has been crossing

over and in front of the opposite pair, and he must reverse that
arrangement; he has been moving sideways with his forehand slightly
leading his quarters. and he must smoothly take his forehand across to lead
in the other direction. Those are the three main things that the horse has to
do in executing a counter-change-of-hand and, although so closely linked
that they appear almost to overlap, they should be tackled individually
and in that order, if the dangers are to be avoided.

The chief dangers are twofold. First, the horse may lose impulsion,
come a little off the bit, and so lose balance and rhythm during the change
of bend or in the moment between the last cross-over stride in one
direction and the first cross-over stride in the new direction. If the rider
tries to execute all three parts of the change by one sudden and
comprehensive shift of his aids, he will be making it almost impossible to
maintain the impulsion throughout. There is just too much to do, and that
applies to both parties. The rider must therefore be careful to break down
his job into its three separate and component parts so that he can watch
over and take care of the impulsion throughout each stage.

The second danger is that the horse, having correctly moved sideways
in one direction – say to the left – with his forehand slightly leading his
quarters, will then start the new movement to the right with the quarters
leading. That of course is incorrect and bad, but it will happen if he has not
been given, or been made to take, the time to transfer his forehand to the
right lead before the quarters are allowed to start in that direction. It is
another fault that is almost bound to occur if the rider tries to do, or
expects his horse to do, everything at once. The rider must refine his aids
until he has time to deal with each stage in its own right. He must know
and fully understand exactly what he has to do and what aids to use to
achieve each of the three aspects of the change, and then put them
together in a smoothly jointed sequence.

Counter-change-of-hand in walk

The proper co-ordination of the rather complicated rein and leg aids in all
counter-changes is so important, and at the same time so intricate, that it is
as well to ensure that the problems are thoroughly sorted out in the walk
before the movement is attempted in trot or canter. The walk is a much
slower and usually much calmer pace than the others, and that gives the
rider adequate time within the strides to experiment with different
variations and degrees of his aids and to discover where his own and his
horse's weaknesses lie. But, even in the walk, the rider must remember

that it is not so much the half-passes that matter – though of course those must certainly be correct – as the smooth, rhythmic flow of the counter-change itself, the transition from one half-pass into the other. Therein lies the skill and the horsemanship, and the results of careful and correct preliminary training. Only when several counter-changes can be performed in walk with activity but with absolute calmness, steadiness and accuracy, should the movement be tried for the first time in trot.

Counter–change–of–hand in trot

The extra momentum and swing of the trot will almost inevitably throw up a few difficulties at first, and not the least of these will be the matter of timing. Performed correctly, there should not be more than one step on a straight line between the two half-passes. That means that the rider must straighten his horse just before he completes the last step of each half-pass, and while so doing he must ensure that the quarters complete the movement to the same alignment as the forehand has done, thus ensuring that the horse is, for an instant, completely parallel to the centre line. To be sure of this, the rider will have to maintain the dominant pressure from his outside leg for a fraction of a second after he has begun to readjust the forehand by straightening with the reins and urging the horse forward with seat and legs into the bit for impulsion. That is perhaps the trickiest part of all. The legs have a lot to do and must remain very steady and relaxed in correct posture.

The next stage is to take the horse smoothly into the new and opposite bend, with just a flicker of shoulder-in at first to ensure that the impulsion is still active and that the quarters are not going to fall in, before finally leading the forehand away into the new half-pass. This may well sound complicated but if it is worked out in this way the rider will be able to retain full control throughout, and a little quiet practice will soon remove the complications.

Faulty aids

As with all forms of half-pass, the rider should be rigorously strict with himself in ensuring that he leads his horse into the lateral movement with a genuinely opening rein. If this is done consistently, it will not only facilitate and improve the result, it will also be a valuable proof of the correct training of the horse and of the training techniques of the rider.

If the horse is going to move to the right, on a curved track or in a lateral movement, it is the opening inside rein that should give him the bend and the direction, the outside rein acting in a controlling and moderating manner. However, it is often very tempting to draw the inside hand inwards and backwards towards the withers in an effort to control the speed at which the forehand is moving laterally or to force the horse into a more accentuated bend. But, in allowing himself to adopt this bad habit, for whatever reason, the rider must have forgotten that in so doing he is exerting an indirect-rein effect, most probably in front of the withers. But, whether in front or behind the withers, it will be positively inhibiting to the direction and fluency of movement that he is trying to produce in his horse (see Figure 6d page 65).

In a good half-pass to the right, the horse should move in that direction with total freedom, especially in the shoulders. Any form of indirect action from the right rein is, in effect, demanding movement of the shoulders to the left, which is contradictory to the requirement. If the indirect action is in front of the withers, it will not only tend to inhibit the movement of the shoulders to the right, but it will also be inducing the quarters to precede the shoulders to the right, which is the last thing we really want to do. In the end, both horse and rider, but particularly the former, will get into a real muddle. The aids will be illogical and inconsistent and will become incomprehensible to the horse, possibly setting up quite serious nervous tensions.

Counter-change in canter

The counter-change in canter is considerably more difficult than in trot. All the same problems found in the exercise at the walk and trot have to be overcome, but in addition we have now to be prepared to grapple with the many things that can so easily go wrong with the flying change of leg that is an integral and essential part of each and every counter-change of direction. On top of that, it is in any case more difficult to maintain balance and collection in the canter. However, all these things mean that the canter counter-change is a fascinating, subtle and rewarding subject for study.

As a preliminary exercise, it is best to perfect the relatively easy figure, (see Figure 9a) preferably in a full-sized arena, of a canter half-pass D–B, with a flying change at B precisely before continuing along the track B–M. We should not attempt even a single counter-change-of-hand until we are confident that we can arrive at the track at B with the horse absolutely parallel to the track – i.e., with his forehand and his quarters hitting the track at the same time – and can then execute a flying change that is full of impulsion and quite straight, or perhaps even with a suggestion of shoulder-in within the actual stride of the change itself. If we have to admit any crookedness in that simple change forward out of the half-pass, we can be certain that the problem will multiply when we try to execute the counter-change which itself involves an acute change of direction. We must also be confident that the horse will perform that simple flying change into the straight line calmly and in balance, without any tendency to plunge forward in a hasty manner. If that should occur, or look like becoming a habit, it may be helpful to bring the horse to a halt a few strides after the change, rein him back calmly for two or three steps, and then continue the canter. It is impossible to do accurate counter-changes if the horse is not calm.

When we are ready to try the first true counter-change-of-hand, we

Figure 8 *Lateral angles*
It is always important that the rider should be aware of the degree of difficulty of the lateral movement he is demanding from his horse; 30° from the original alignment should seldom be exceeded even with an advanced horse. The maximum required in the Olympic Grand Prix or Grand Prix Special in trot or canter is 40°

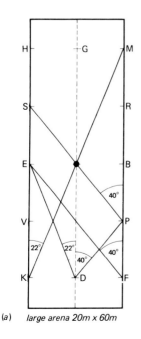

(a)   large arena 20m x 60m

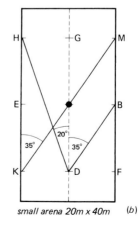

small arena 20m x 40m   (b)

should limit the exercise to one single counter-change, consisting of a right half-pass D–B, followed immediately by a left half-pass B–G, and incorporating one flying change of leg from right to left at B (see Figure 9a). That is a canter counter-change in its simplest and easiest form. In the early stages, the rider should take special care not to force the first stride of the new half-pass B–G, as this can easily jeopardize the fluency and impulsion of the flying change of leg. That in turn may alarm the horse and cause him to begin jumping to the side when, on other occasions, the rider is trying to do perfectly straightforward changes.

When we first attempt the single counter-change, we can expect to find it comparatively easy because there will be plenty of room, at least in the big arena, to fit in the two half-passes at easy angles. We shall consequently be able to allow ourselves the licence of a straight stride or two on the track either immediately before or immediately after the change of leg. The straight stride immediately after the flying change will give us the opportunity to reorganize and recollect ourselves for the new half-pass. But soon we shall want to perform that change so as to link the two half-passes as tidily and as exactly as necessary when executing the whole series of counter-changes normally called for in competitions on either side of the centre line.

In all competition work, as well as in all formal displays, the counter-changes-of-hand in canter have to be done with a precise and pre-specified number of strides in each leg of the movement. Starting at D, for example, on the right lead, the requirement may be for four strides to the right, followed by eight to the left (four on each side of the centre line), then eight to the right, and finally four to the left, completing the movement at G (see Figure 9b). The centre line will have been crossed twice, and three counter-changes-of-hand will have been executed, one at each point of the zigzag course from D to G involving relatively easy angles of 27 degrees. At the highest level of international competition, five counter-changes with three strides on each side of the centre line are required and this means that each half-pass must be executed at an angle of 30 degrees. This compares with the greater angle of 40 degrees when the half-pass is executed as a traversaal, right across the arena from S to P, or the equivalent, in both trot and canter, as occurs in the Grand Prix Special test (see Figure 8a).

The more counter-changes the rider tries to fit into the restricted length of any arena, the more severe the angles will become and the greater the difficulties for the horse. Great care must be taken not to demand too much of him in this way, and it is well to remember that there is a wide

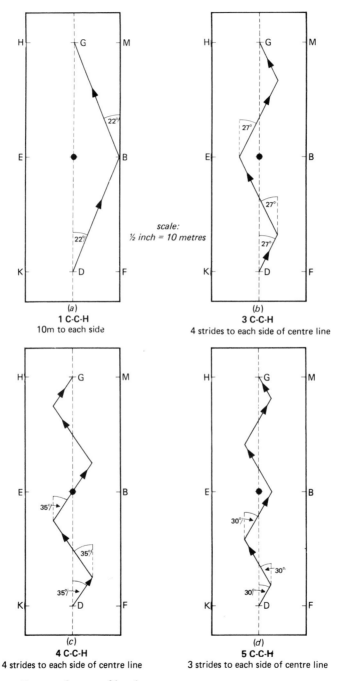

scale:
½ inch = 10 metres

(a)
1 C-C-H
10m to each side

(b)
3 C-C-H
4 strides to each side of centre line

(c)
4 C-C-H
4 strides to each side of centre line

(d)
5 C-C-H
3 strides to each side of centre line

Figure 9 *Counter-changes-of-hand*

Two counter-changes in canter. (a) The horse has been half-passing to the right, and here changes leg directly into left half-pass; (b) after the left half-pass, the horse changes leg into right half-pass. The bend is correct for the new direction. In both cases note the

stability of the rider's position and the control of the new direction effected by his inside   *b*
leg. Both pictures show how the initiating hindleg delivers the whole of the lateral thrust
for the new sideways canter stride. Reiner Klimke on Dux

difference between the angles involved in moving from the quarter marker to X, or vice versa, in the 20 × 40-metre arena and the same route in the 20 × 60-metre arena. In the former case, the angle of 35 degrees is quite severe, whereas in the bigger arena it is relatively light at 22 degrees.

Major problems for the rider

The problems confronting the rider in trying to execute a correct and satisfactory counter-change in canter require a lot of thought and study if he is to avoid muddles and the possibility of unnerving himself or his horse. To make it easier to explain, we will consider in detail the single counter-change (D–B–G), carried out with as much finesse as if it were one of a compact series of three, four or five, in which there would be no room for licence or poor timing. And we will consider only the last four steps of the half-pass that precedes the change of leg, as if we were riding the first leg of a series starting from the centre line.

In theory, it is perfectly possible for a horse, moving in a very collected and well-balanced manner, to complete a prescribed number of strides –say four – to the right, make his flying change of leg in the air and, as part of the change, make the first of the prescribed number of steps to the left. He will have made four *full* strides to the right followed immediately by four *full* strides to the left. Almost the whole of the thrust that impels the horse sideways in a canter half-pass emanates from the one hindleg that initiates the stride – that is to say, the left hindleg when the half-pass is to the right. Then on completion of that stride, when all four legs are off the ground, the change takes place; the right hindleg comes to the ground first and alone, to initiate the first stride of the new canter-left and, simultaneously, if the balance and collection are good enough, to thrust the body and all the other limbs (the latter still ungrounded) to the left into the first stride of the left half-pass.

The ideal

That, in essence, would be the perfect counter-change in canter, assuming that the other factors such as the bends, the straightness and the impulsion were equally satisfactory. The last stride to the right and the first to the left will both have been full ones, in every way equal to those that preceded or followed them. This is possible, but in practice it is extremely difficult and demands such an exceptionally high standard of horsemanship and equine dexterity that most trainers and judges are prepared to settle for something a little easier and consequently, in all probability, more pleasing to the eye. The compromise is usually arrived at by allowing for one completely straight stride either immediately before or during the change of leg, the former being the most common.

The compromise

In practice, therefore, when four strides to either side of the centre line are required, only three full strides in half-pass are usually shown, followed by the fourth stride straight ahead. The latter is followed by the flying change which itself forms the first stride of the half-pass in the new direction. The alternative option is to ride four full strides in the original half-pass, followed by a flying change straight ahead, to be followed by the first stride of the new half-pass – though in fact that stride will have to count as the second of that leg of four.

It is unnecessary to be too dogmatic about which of the two alternative and compromise methods of riding the counter-change should be used. There are circumstances in which, at least for a time, the second method becomes the most advantageous – for instance, if the horse has developed a habit of jumping to the side when asked to make a flying change on a straight line. This can easily happen if the counter-changes are introduced before the straightness and impulsion of changes on a straight line have been thoroughly established. He may jump to the side as an anticipation of a counter-change, or merely as a means of evading the stresses of the straight-through impulsion required in an ordinary change. In either case, the greatest danger lies in the rider's inability to ride a straight change when he wants one, and overcoming that must be given priority over all other problems connected with counter-changes. The key to problems of this nature lies in the finesse that the rider has achieved in the use of his aids for flying changes. In the long run, as we will discuss in the next chapter, straight changes are best ridden by using the seatbone as the dominant aid, leaving the legs mainly busy with maintaining the impulsion and with demanding the jump to the side in the case of a counter-change.

It is of course important that the amount of ground covered by each canter stride should be the same in both directions so that the zigzag remains symmetrical in relation to the centre line.

9

Sequence Flying Changes of Leg

It is tempting to suggest that sequence (or tempi) flying changes, which are flying changes made after a small and prescribed number of strides between each change, will present no great difficulty. Such a statement would be true enough if it could be assumed that the performance of horse and rider in the single changes was of a really high order – that is to say, that they were consistently straight, fluent, collected, calm, impulsive and free from resistance. Most riders will have to admit that their changes do not always live up to those splendid ideals, and so they find that putting changes together in tempi sequences serves all too often to show up the weaknesses that existed, but were more easily camouflaged, in the singles.

Nevertheless, it is a fact that sequence changes, whether in four-, three-, two- or one-time sequences, are not skills that have to be taught to the horse as new exercises in their own right. All that is needed is to improve the singles so that their frequency can be increased without additional worry. You do not set out one morning to teach a horse the trick of doing two-time changes when previously he has only done them in three-time. All you have to do, provided the time is ripe, is to ask for the next change one stride earlier than you have done before.

Sequence changes are in essence precisely the same as the single variety; the only problem is that, as the number of strides between changes is reduced, there is less and less time in which to rectify any errors that have arisen in the canter as a result of the previous change of leg. Some of those errors may be so small that they will be hardly visible to the spectator, but the rider will feel and be inconvenienced by them, and the inconvenience will be sufficient to make the subsequent change more difficult. They include: a slight loss of balance or collection; a swing of the quarters or other lack of straightness; perhaps a slight coming behind the bit; a flattening or tensing of the horse's back; or some momentary unlevelness or resistance in the mouth. These and similar problems are always liable to occur because the sudden physical effort required to execute the change tends to show up and even to magnify any latent imperfections that already exist in the canter. And the long list of potential weaknesses in the horse's performance will almost certainly be matched by those of the rider himself, who may stiffen his back, grip or raise his knees, get in front of the movement, lose his seat, lower his head and generally fall short of his own good intentions.

With single changes it may often be possible for the rider to postpone the change for a stride or two if he feels that by so doing he will be able to prepare his horse more satisfactorily. And any troubles that arise from the single change can be quietly smoothed out, without upsetting or wrestling with the horse, during the subsequent canter. But corrections of any kind become much more difficult, and require a much higher degree of equestrian skill and tact, when each change has at all costs to be made on the last of a specified number of strides, and when only that restricted number of strides is available for the business of rectification.

Timing the aids

Without doubt, the most common source of imperfections in the changes is the untimeliness of the rider's aids – an aspect that should always be his first concern when things do not go quite right. Because of the inevitable increase in tensions set up by the physiological pressures that we have already outlined in connection with sequence changes, it is more important than ever that the aids for each consecutive change should be given in good time and perhaps even a little earlier than would usually be done for a single. It is the late aid that causes the horse to get flustered or to despair of being able to give the answer that he knows is expected of him. And, as the number of strides between the changes is reduced, and as the rider consequently becomes more and more pressed for time to make the necessary corrections in his horse and in his own posture, so he will find it more difficult to avoid being a little late with his aids for the next change. But practice, more practice and yet more practice, combined with sympathy for the horse and an awareness of the problems he has to overcome, and the patience to go back a step or two to get to the roots of any major fault, will bring a satisfactory result in the end.

The question of timing is especially important with young horses and must always be carefully watched. Its significance applies to all the aids, not least to the new inside leg, and the horse should be given the best possible chance, despite other preoccupations connected with corrections from the rider, to absorb the message and to produce a change in good form. If the signals come through to him just a trifle too late in the stride for the thing to be done easily, he will no doubt make a supreme effort to make the change, but the chances are that it will be a bad one. It will be jerky; the new inside hindleg will not swing properly through; the quarters will swing inwards to ease the problem for the inside leg; or the horse will dwell in the change and drop behind the bit. The rider will feel these things happening and, being disappointed, may then, if he is lacking in experience or humility, chase or abuse the horse that has done its best under nearly impossible circumstances.

If that kind of situation is allowed to recur too often, there will be a grave danger of the horse losing confidence in himself and in his rider, and then out of desperation developing the habit of making a faulty change in one of the ways suggested every time the action is called for and even when, later on, the aids are correctly applied. If that happens, it is advisable to go right back to square one and to go through the processes of teaching the single changes all over again as if they were part of a new lesson being taught for the first time. Success will be quicker that way, especially for the not-so-experienced rider, who will thereby have the opportunity to check and revise his own techniques. So – rider, question thyself.

Aids

We have spoken of all the aids for the changes, implying that there are change aids of importance besides the conventional leg aids. The latter are certainly the most powerful, and can command the greatest respect, and it is for that reason that riders often tend to rely on them almost exclusively when first initiating a young horse into the art of flying changes, and probably for quite a long time thereafter. But riders eventually come to realize that the leg aids, though undoubtedly powerful, are not necessarily the most subtle aids and can all too easily become rather crude. As the need for subtlety increases with the frequency of the sequence changes, so the intelligent rider will increasingly search for, and will ultimately give predominance to, other and more discreet methods of signalling in order to ensure timeliness. Once the horse has understood and accepted the basic technique of changing the sequence of his legs in canter, with precision and on request, there will be no great difficulty in achieving good changes by means other than the legs and seat. It will be found that they can be made by the use of the reins alone; by a combination of the reins and seat; or, most usefully, by the seat alone in conjunction with a unilateral bracing of the back.

Leg aids

Normally, leg aids involve some degree of signal from the seat, since each leg, for all practical purposes, begins at the seatbone on the same side. Nevertheless, it is perfectly possible to cause a flying change by the use of the lower legs acting entirely on their own, without any influence whatever from the seat – if, for example, the rider chooses to do the exercise while standing up in his stirrups. One famous double Olympic gold medallist used at one time to do all his one-time changes in that manner, thereby ensuring complete freedom of his horse's back. His changes certainly showed great fluency, albeit somewhat at the expense of collection.

Rein aids

Changes created by means of the reins alone are in line with the French theory that all equestrian progress aims in the long run at keeping the legs free to concentrate solely on the all-important problem of maintaining impulsion, while leaving the reins to deal with the bend and the direction. There is much to be said for this philosophy if it is practised with sufficient skill and sophistication, though it does carry with it, especially when applied to changes of leg, the risk of the rein aids becoming too heavy and obtrusive, thus defeating the impulsive work of the legs and disturbing the horse.

It is quite common for the hands and reins to play a significant part in a mixed package of aids for changes. They can be used to give the horse a guide into the new flexion just before, or simultaneously with, the main leg or seat request for the change. They can be used to give the horse a little lift on the side of the new leading leg, to delay its descent to the ground. But, in the end, most riders tend to succumb to the temptation to overdo the rein aids, causing more harm than good, and it is probably wiser to decide from the outset that the reins and hands shall do nothing, or as little as possible. This is especially important when riding the very difficult one-time changes, in which it is vital to avoid all inessential

a

In all changes of leg, the rider's seat should remain firmly in the saddle, with no twist in the body, to effect and push through the change. (a) Shows the change being signalled by the rider's left leg. The near hindleg will now come forward before the off hindleg, to initiate the canter right; (b) shows the change completed. The rider's hip-bones and stomach are pressed forward to lead the torso into the movement and to accompany the 'jump'. Note correct position of whip and consequently also of the hands. The author on Peter Jones

movement of any kind. In these, the nicety of balance is so delicate that it can be destroyed by a gratuitous tug on the mouth, particularly as no change of flexion is required.

Seat aids

We should, however, consider very carefully the method of making our changes by the use of the seat aids alone, by which we mean the influence of the seatbones reinforced by a braced, though still supple, back. Let it be quite clear that there is no absolute necessity to do this, although it is a method that, for those who master it, greatly enhances the quality of their horsemanship. The advantages of this method are as follows: the legs are left free to care mainly for the impulsion that is such a vital part of all good flying changes; it virtually rules out the possibility of the rider's seat leaving the saddle, as so often happens to an undesirable and unsightly extent when too much reliance is placed on the leg aids; it helps to keep the horse 'in front of the rider'; and it is most unlikely to degenerate into crudity, as can so easily happen with either the legs or the reins. In short, the use of the seat alone to produce flying changes comes nearer to the ideal than any alternative method used by itself. Its study and practice is most strongly recommended.

We should, however, remember that ideal changes will occur, whatever the aids, only out of ideal conditions. And, as there are so many little things that can arise to cause the condition of the horse at any given moment to be somewhat less than ideal, the best riders will probably find that it is quite frequently necessary to compromise by calling in their legs to assist their seat. But it can be taken as axiomatic that some use of the seatbones will invariably be complementary and beneficial to the leg aids and will reduce the extent to which the latter are necessary, thereby increasing the subtlety of the aids as a whole. When all is said, the aids have to be regarded as a whole. The rider has two hands, two seatbones and two legs. None of them can be ignored and each of them has a part to play, either positive or negative, in the overall harmony.

The technique for using the seat as the dominant aid for flying changes may need some explanation for those who have not experienced it. The left canter, for example, is initiated and maintained largely by the influence of the left seatbone which, with each stride, thrusts forward slightly in advance of, and more positively than, the right seatbone – all in conformity with the natural slight bend or flexion of the horse to the left in that canter. When the rider wishes to change to the canter right he will, at the appropriate moment, when the horse is about to have all four feet off the ground, change the sequence and influence of his seatbones from right–left to left–right, the right seatbone now taking the more positive and advanced position. By doing this, and by putting the predominant and forward influence into the right seatbone, the rider will be encouraging the horse to follow well through with the fore- and hindlegs on that side and at the same time to flex slightly to the right, thus assuming the canter right. In the process, the rider will have had to make his left seatbone exert its influence twice in quick succession, just before the actual change, and that will have played its part in causing the horse to make two successive beats with his left hindleg, as must happen in order to initiate the change into the canter right. This underlines the harmony that can and must exist between the rider's seatbones and his horse's quarters and hindlegs.

The detailed explanation given in the preceding paragraph may seem a little complicated, but we can perhaps summarize the essence of the matter by saying that the rider demands his flying change by pressing forward in the saddle his new inside seat- and hipbones, this being accomplished by a strong unilateral bracing of the back on that side. That is not particularly difficult to do and is surprisingly effective, provided the rider remembers that it is, as always, the stomach and the surrounding bone structure of the pelvis that must lead the body forward into each successive stride. That factor is most important in ensuring that the rider does not get 'in front of the movement' and, to the same end, he must take special pains not to look down in the direction of his hands or the horse's shoulder, since any forward inclination of the head, or hollowing of the chest, must inevitably tip his weight and disturb the harmony of his balance with that of the horse. There is also a relation between the position of the head and the requirement already noted that the hipbone, or top of the pelvis, must be pressed forward as well as the seatbone and even slightly in advance of the latter. This will happen anyway if the back is correctly braced, but it is stressed here as a reminder of the importance of not collapsing the lower spine during the change. The forward action of the hipbone has the effect of increasing the power of the seatbone without making it heavy, whereas any backward collapse of the lumbar spine deadens and inhibits the flow of movement.

One-time changes

One-time changes are a special case that calls for very detailed and intensive study. Perhaps we ought not to regard them as special, since in many respects they share precisely the same problems and require the same treatment and approach as the four-, three- and two-time changes. But there is one respect in which the one-timers are distinct from the others: quite simply, they present the ultimate difficulty in regard to the timing of the aids and the balance in motion of the horse and rider.

The usual requirements of balance of the horse, balance of the rider, maintaining impulsion and soft submission, responsiveness to the aids, sheer gymnastic dexterity, subtlety in applying the aids, all remain pertinent, but now permit virtually no margin of error. In all the other tempi changes there is at least one free stride in which the horse and rider have the chance to regain the equilibrium and overall physical control that may have deteriorated to a greater or lesser degree during the previous change. But now, if the horse is to succeed in one-time changes, he has to land into each successive stride with virtually perfect balance and, without any hesitation or loss of impulsion, take off again immediately into the following change, back on to the lead he has just forsaken, with equally perfect balance, and to go on doing it.

When well performed, the one-time changes feel beautiful and look beautiful. They even look easy, but there is no shadow of doubt that they involve a very unusual degree of muscular control and also of mental effort for the horse, in the course of which he can enjoy no respite. Neither

Figure 10 *Flying change of leg*
The act of a flying change of leg in the canter occurs when the horse, after cantering left as shown in drawings 1 to 3 and in the brief moment of total suspension that follows the completion of the stride that began with the right hindleg (drawings 1 to 4), changes the sequence of his hindlegs so as to begin the next stride with the other (left) hindleg. He thus initiates the first stride of the canter right (drawings 5 to 8) (Drawings by Patricia Frost)

left lead

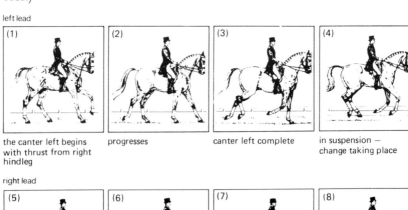

the canter left begins   progresses   canter left complete   in suspension —
with thrust from right   change taking place
hindleg

right lead

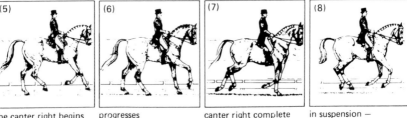

the canter right begins   progresses   canter right complete   in suspension —
with thrust from left
hindleg

A fine picture of the first beat (off hindleg) of a new left lead in a one-time sequence. It demonstrates clearly the high degree of balance and energetic activity required to perform this movement well. Jennie Loriston-Clarke on Dutch Courage

can the rider, and it is the latter's job to set going and then to maintain the necessary degree of mutual concentration and activity to achieve successful continuity.

Everyone will know and enjoy the sight of a young child gaily dancing along a street pavement doing one-time changes, more usually called skipping. The action seems to come naturally to all children the world over, without any tuition or difficulty. But the child is fortunate in that the weight of the body is carried directly above the hindquarters and loins. For the horse, everything is much more difficult and much more of an effort, because the great weight of the major part of his body lies directly in front of, instead of above, the lifting and thrusting mechanism of the quarters and loins. It is clear that such a precise, high-pressured and continuously buoyant movement must tax any horse to the limits of his ability, and that a very high level of equestrian dexterity will be required from the rider. For example, if the rider, in his efforts to create or recreate impulsion after the beginning of a series of one-times, should allow the weight of his upper body or even his head to get in front of his own centre of balance, he will inevitably unbalance himself and his horse, thus making it virtually impossible for the latter to take off for the next change. For this reason alone, it is essential that the rider should have developed a seat that is at all times firm and totally independent of his leg and hand movements, or else he will be unable to operate with sufficient immediacy and accuracy. In particular, the arms and shoulders must be relaxed so that the hands can be free, light and sensitive for their multiple tasks of controlling excessive impulsion, guiding or regaining direction, and allowing the forward impulsion to flow without interruption from one change into the next. To control but also to allow is probably the most difficult of the rider's tasks. And, more than on all other occasions, it is important that the legs never lose contact with the horse's sides. It is that contact that gives immediacy to the rider's feel, to his understanding of the changing situation, and to the corrective aids.

Aid application

Exactly how the various aids should be applied will vary in many details with each horse and possibly with each rider, depending on such things as the standard of preparatory training, of temperament and sensitivity, and of the rider's previous experience. Each rider must feel his way by trial and error towards the best solution for the day and for each horse he trains, and even then he may well find it profitable to make certain adjustments as the horse's training progresses or suffers setbacks. This will not be too difficult provided he remembers the main principles and constantly checks that he is not violating them. He must watch the vital point of never being late with his aids, and of never being over-demanding. And above all, if he is to avoid long-term failure, he must be able to maintain his correct or near-perfect rider position despite all the difficulties that occur beneath his saddle.

Provided the horse is light and supple, one-time changes can in due course be performed on a large circle, or in serpentines or loops, as well as on straight lines. Naturally, these are more difficult than straight-line exercises because it is considerably more difficult to maintain a consistent balance when changing into or out of the counter canter. It is not a bad idea to ensure that horse and rider can perform three-time changes with ease on a circle before attempting two-times on the straight; and that they can perform two-times on the circle before attempting one-times on the straight.

Any troubles that occur in the initial stages of teaching one-times to a young horse will usually be attributable to lack of confidence on the part of the horse and, even more probably, on the part of the rider. Long before the time comes to begin the work, both parties should have become well versed and confident in making changes at almost any time or place, but the unbroken sequence of bounces required in one-times can be very confusing at first and must be tackled with great patience and tact, though firmly and without hesitation.

The danger of overtaxing the horse's confidence with one-time changes dictates the method of approaching the early stages of the work. It is best to start by using the long side of an enclosed arena where the horse will obtain some moral support from the wall or fence. Then ensure, with some repetition, that he will confidently make a single change from the inside to the outside lead, towards the wall, and will do so from very light and discreet aids. Then, from an inside lead, and early on one of the long side tracks, ask the horse to do his first double change, a one-two in one-time, so that he will end up back on the inside lead on which he should be allowed to canter straight on in an easy manner with much neck-patting. If that initial effort is successful, the exercise should be repeated several times, but always at precisely the same spot on the track. That will be enough for the first day.

After a week or two, when the horse will perform that initial one-two quite calmly at various places on the track, it will be time to begin the reverse one-two on the other rein, in a similar manner. The next stage will be to begin speeding up the frequency of the one-two changes until they are performed at least twice on each long side of a small arena.

It will then be time to ask for a one-two-three, and this is best done by working from an initial outside lead so that the action will finish once more on the comfortable inside lead. From then on it will become a matter of steadily but quietly building on the mutual confidence and shared harmony of both partners to increase the number of changes, little by little, like adding daisies to a daisy chain. It is, however, very important that the rider should not ask for more changes than the horse seems able to perform with calmness and without getting into a muddle. And of course it may easily be the rider who gets into a muddle with his aids. It is one thing to ride one-time changes on a well-trained horse, but quite another to ride them on a horse that is in the process of being trained. The latter requires the exercise of great patience, combined with very skilfully co-ordinated aids that will only be possible if the rider has a firm seat, quiet hands and still legs.

One of the main difficulties for the rider, throughout the development of one-time changes, is to maintain collection from one change to the next, together with the necessary impulsive engagement of the quarters. If these qualities are lost it becomes almost impossible for the horse to continue the sequence. Here once more, as in so many other instances, success depends on the ability of the rider to keep his horse in front of his seat and legs under difficult or adverse circumstances. Only if he can do this will he be able to assist his horse as the latter tries to master this very delicately balanced movement.

In this connection it is particularly important to ensure that the stride of the first change in the sequence is full and generous. If the first change is short, and consequently a bit quick, the rider's aid for the second is liable to be late and thus inharmonious. Alternatively, in his subsequent efforts to give his aids in good time for the second change, the rider may cause his horse to become uncertain as to whether he had really been asked to change at all and so lose confidence in the first one to the extent of failing to complete it with the front legs. A full stride in the first place will provide sufficient time to obviate these difficulties.

These one-time changes inevitably put a lot of pressure on the horse's capacity for thought and co-ordination, and this can easily cause him to become anxious and tensed up. Over-anxiety can become a great danger and may create all sorts of nervous upsets that will sometimes react on the much simpler four, three or two-time changes. Every precaution must therefore be taken to develop the lesson step by step, and with calmness as the motto.

It is usually helpful and wise to avoid practising changes too frequently on the diagonal of an arena, or even on the long side of a small or 40-metre arena. The diagonal in particular quickly becomes too obvious for the horse, with the result that he will become tense the moment he is turned on to it; and nervous tension breeds mistakes and anticipations. At certain stages of training an open field or grass trackway can be ideal for practising sequence changes.

The urge felt by every dressage rider to perfect the art of tempi flying changes is a most natural and irresistible one, and will not be satisfied until one-times can be performed with apparent ease for quite long distances such as, for example, once round a 20-metre circle or for 60, 70 or even 100 yards on a straight line in a field. Such can be the culminating pleasure of one of the most fascinating studies in the dressage curriculum. Flying changes are not intrinsically difficult, yet they are virtually never totally free of latent problems that have to be watched or ironed out in order to maintain the smooth path towards perfection. Thus they constitute a lifetime's study of very great interest.

As a final word of advice for riding good sequence-changes, and more particularly one-time changes, the rider must endeavour

a Never to let his shoulders get in front of his seat.
b To keep his seatbones on the saddle.
c To keep his loins supple and swinging forward with the movement.
d To keep his toes to the front and the inside of his lower-leg in continuous contact with the horse.
e To restrict any backward-and-forward movement of the lower-leg to the absolute minimum. Such movement should hardly be visible.
f To make each demand for a change with one harmonious action comprising the loin, seat, thighs, knees and lower-leg. Any lack of harmony or harshness of the aids will be reflected at once in the horse's actions.

10

Canter Pirouettes

The essence of a good canter pirouette lies, as with so many other difficult movements, in lively impulsion and collection. In the pirouette, these two qualities are required in the highest degree, with particular stress on the word 'lively' in its relation to the actual lifting of the feet off the ground.

In its basic form, the canter pirouette is a short canter half-pass on a very small circle. To perform such a movement, the horse has to be in maximum collection to the extent that he appears to be more or less squatting or, in the German dressage parlance, '*Gesetzen*' (sitting down). He lowers his haunches so as to make the forehand sufficiently light to be brought round on the outer, and therefore longer, track of the circle while remaining in a properly co-ordinated three-, or nearly three-, beat canter. Many authorities state that it is virtually impossible for the true three-beat footfall to be retained throughout a pirouette and that slow-motion films indicate that it is never achieved, even though the degree of collection is such that the break into four-time is hardly discernible to the naked eye. But the true canter form remains the ideal, and any major divergence into four-time must be criticized, particularly if it reaches the stage when the horse appears to be lifting its forehand round the more or less static hindlegs in a strenuous, heaving manner. Both ends of the horse must appear to be operating together, as a unit, in a continuous canter rhythm and in virtually the same tempo as the canter out of which the pirouette developed.

The photograph opposite gives an almost ideal impression of a canter pirouette; the only question is whether the off or leading foreleg has left the ground before the arrival on the ground of the near hind foot that is initiating the next stride. Has there been a moment of total suspension

The quintessence of a canter pirouette. The horse rounds his back to 'sit down', with well engaged and flexed hindlegs, to carry almost the whole of his weight on his haunches, enabling the forehand to turn lightly round the pivot. Harry Boldt on Woyceck

between the two strides? At the same time, there appears no reason to doubt that the sequence is in three-time, which is possible even without the correct moment of full suspension, since it depends entirely on whether or not the second beat is correctly formed by the diagonals – in this case the off hind and near fore. Probably only a fast sequence of cine pictures taken on a hard and bare surface can prove or disprove the absolute correctness of a good pirouette, and for ordinary purposes it will be sufficient to concentrate on the overall impression created within the main requirements of a lively, impulsive, collected and rhythmical canter. In the picture, the general posture and balance of both horse and rider are beyond criticism and it is probable that nothing better is ever achieved.

Controls

The key to riding a canter pirouette lies in the complete control by the rider of each single canter stride made by the horse in the course of the movement. The relationship between horse and rider, and the control exercised, should be such that the rider is confident of his ability to adjust, speed up, slow down, re-collect, stop or re-start the canter strides at will, according to the needs of the moment as presented by the horse in his efforts to do this difficult exercise. The rider must feel and be aware of each step as a unit in its own right. He must not allow himself to get into a situation in which, once he has begun a pirouette, he has so little detailed control that he has to complete it for better or worse, at whatever speed or with whatever number of steps that the horse decides. If that occurs, as it very easily can, the rider has quite simply lost control, and is no longer the dominant partner. And it will follow as a certainty that the exit from the pirouette will also lack control.

The degree of control of the horse's strides required within the pirouette itself must also be exercised during the approach and also, with equal finesse, during the exit on to the chosen straight line or into whatever movement is to follow. The rider must be able to stop or start the movement at any moment or, if he is dissatisfied with the feel, to ride out of it in a well-collected manner at any point. And, as implied at the beginning of this chapter, that kind of control is only possible to the extent to which the rider can maintain impulsive and lively collection.

To press on with a bad pirouette – one that is perhaps ill-balanced, poorly collected or hurried – is always bad policy, since the horse will soon develop the habit of throwing himself around in a hurried and unrhythmic tempo, on the forehand, or above the bit with a hollow back.

The start of a canter pirouette. The horse is a little hollow (compare with photograph on page 113) but clearly shows the important element of shoulder-in that ensures the correct relationship between quarters and forehand, with the inside hindleg well controlled. Good rider position. Jennie Loriston-Clarke on Dutch Courage

Any of these weaknesses are almost bound to lead to some sort of tussle between the two partners, with the result that the horse will begin to be frightened of the movement and will lose his calm. Thereafter, the first indication from the rider that a pirouette is required will put the horse into a fluster – a habit which is hard to cure and will always impede good work.

Lateral controls

Under the heading of controls we must consider one supremely important factor in riding pirouettes. The rider must ensure and insist on total lateral control of his horse's quarters; this implies complete and unhesitating submission and obedience from the horse – a matter which should be thoroughly established long before he is introduced to the special stresses of the pirouette. The true meaning and significance of that obedience will then be apparent and will become essential. We have already noted that the pirouette is, in essence, a tight canter half-pass on a small circle, and it has to be ridden as such. The absolute control of the quarters is vital in any half-pass, and never more so than when it is executed on a circle, and a tight one at that. This control, in fact, becomes the rider's chief concern. He has to be satisfied that, with each stride, the hindlegs will step, still in their correct canter sequence and with plenty of forward impulsion, just a tiny bit to the side to which the pirouette is being made. In the left pirouette, they must make ground by an inch or so to the left – or to the right in a right pirouette. This is not easy, but it can and must be done. And if in the early stages, by moving the quarters inwards and to the side, the pirouette becomes bigger than was intended, that will constitute a much lesser fault than if the quarters had drifted outwards and against the rider's outside-leg control.

The significance of this aspect of pirouette control lies in the natural tendency of the horse to make any tight turn by pivoting on his centre. Left to themselves, and because the greater part of the weight is placed by nature on the forehand, the quarters will tend to fly out, thus relieving the strain on the loins and haunches. But if that is permitted the horse will lose most of his collection, ending up with too much weight on his forehand and quite unprepared and unable to make an efficient and controlled getaway. The quarters must be made to form the true pivot and must be kept with and under the movement.

Aids

Outside-leg aids

The bases for the rider's control of the quarters throughout the pirouette are his outside seatbone and leg, which are effectively part and parcel of the same aid effect. If the weight is allowed to come off the outside seatbone the rider will be leaning inwards, putting too much weight on the inside seatbone and thereby tending to push his horse towards the outside of the circle. That, of course, is directly contrary to what he is trying to do, which is to cause the horse to move towards the inside in a half-pass manner.

To avoid the outward drift, the rider must also hold his body strictly in line with the vertical plane of his horse's centre of gravity, guarding against the tendency to lean forward as the speed of the horse's advance is reduced to zero, and keeping a full share of the weight on that outside seatbone. A firmly positioned seatbone acts as an anchor for the action of the whole of his outside leg which, if the heel is then thrust well down towards the ground as well as being kept firmly against the horse behind the girth, becomes a very powerful tool for maintaining the slight sideways movement of the quarters towards the direction of the pirouette. Achieving the correct and most effective position of the body is facilitated if the rider continues to look ahead over his horse's ears but turns a little to the inside from his waist upwards.

It should be noted here that the outside leg has the intricate tasks of controlling the quarters, helping to maintain impulsion, and helping to turn the middle and front end of the horse around the pivot of the quarters. The precise position of this leg must be discovered by experiment with each particular horse.

Inside-leg aids

It must not be forgotten that the inside leg has an important job to do as well, notwithstanding the effort to make maximum use of the outside one. The inside leg has the dual role of maintaining the impulsion and activity of the canter and of controlling the speed at which the horse actually turns around the circle. To put it another way, the inside leg either checks or allows the turn of the forehand during the pirouette. It acts in this way for each stride in turn, and the horse should be trained to wait for permission from the inside leg to make each successive step round the circle. Failure of the inside leg to exercise this control, or the horse's disobedience of its instructions, will almost invariably result in the horse throwing himself around in an untidy and hurried manner that will destroy the rhythm of the movement. And, as with all canter work, the inside seatbone works in conjunction with the whole of the leg, pressing forward in the saddle a little in front of the outside one, the heel lowering a little towards the ground with each stride.

The production of a good canter pirouette will depend, above all else, on the effective interplay of the rider's inside and outside legs, and on his skill in using the one to counterbalance the effect of the other.

Rein aids

There are also the reins to be considered in connection with the controls of a pirouette. It might be thought that they would have to play a major part in a movement involving such an acute change of direction, but in fact this is not the case, or at least it is not at all desirable, for two reasons. First, rein action can all too easily disturb the balance and concentration of the horse and, second, any effort by the rider to make the acute turn mainly by using the inside rein will tend to create too much bend in the neck, to the detriment of impulsion. It would also at the same time accentuate the natural tendency of the quarters to drift outwards.

The inside rein: In practice, the rider should endeavour to restrict the action of the inside rein to ensure that the horse remains round, soft in the mouth, and slightly flexed in that direction, the strength of contact being reduced to the minimum. The horse will then be able to concentrate on finding his own way round the pirouette without anxiety about his balance being disturbed by pulls at his mouth. Both hands should be kept close together and as still as possible.

The outside rein: The outside rein assumes the role, as in virtually every other movement, of exerting the dominant control. In this case, its chief purpose is to contain the impulsion so as to reduce the forward motion and, at the same time, by an indirect or sideways pressure on the neck, to assist in turning the horse, stride by stride, around the pirouette at the required speed. In the latter task it will be complemented and assisted by the outside leg in a combined lateral-aid effect.

The rider's back

We cannot leave this discussion about the aids for the pirouette without mention of the very special significance attached to the correct use and posture of the rider's back. The action of the back, loins and pelvis is always important but is crucial in this case. In the pirouette we need: maximum collection in order to make the horse light enough to execute such a restricted movement; enough impulsion to convert into a totally lateral movement; and maximum activity in order to maintain the action of the heavily loaded hindlegs. All these things call for exceptionally active, effective and sympathetic riding techniques if the horse is to receive the messages in acceptable form. Such techniques can only stem from a superlative seat control, which the rider must be able to maintain in defiance of whatever problems arise. To keep his seat secure and effective under the testing conditions of the pirouette, the rider must keep his loins well braced and the top of his pelvis or hipbones, together with his stomach, pushed well forward towards his hands to the extent that his shoulders may be slightly behind the normal vertical line of his torso. It is of no great concern if he thus appears to be leaning back, because the forward thrust of the hipbones will ensure that the weight is being carried forward and down, towards the front of the saddle where it is wanted, and not backwards where it would inconvenience the horse. In that position, the rider can remain impervious to and unmoved by any sudden loss of impulsion or 'drawing back' by the horse. He will be able to keep his mount in front of him and will be correctly positioned to make the necessary corrections.

Conversely, if the rider allows his shoulders to get in front of his seat and his loins to collapse, the smallest deviation in speed or direction by the horse is likely to cause him to lose his seat altogether and, for all practical purposes, he will have lost control of the situation. His best chance of avoiding that indignity is to ride into and through the pirouette with his loins well braced and his stomach well advanced. If any visual proof of that theory is needed, it will be found in photographs of all the leading dressage riders in the world.

Preparation work

Every trainer, however experienced, has to spend a long time, probably many months, in preparing his young horse for pirouette work. He will use all kinds of exercises, many of them only indirectly connected with the ultimate aim that he has in mind, but all concerned with loosening, flexing and strengthening the muscles and joints of the hindlegs so that the horse will be fit when the time comes to begin working on the pirouette itself. Among the many exercises that will be helpful in the preparatory stage are: repeated short strike-offs from the walk or the halt; half-halts and halts; rein-backs; canter travers; and canter shoulder-ins. The first and the last three of these will yield the most direct dividends. The travers performed on a large circle is a particularly valuable early exercise in this context since, by forcing the front legs to take larger steps than the hindlegs, it tends to lighten the forehand.

Travers and renvers

A number of books by famous trainers lay special stress on the value of the canter travers and renvers as being the best exercises for the actual lead into the young horse's first efforts at a few pirouette steps. They recommend the travers ridden on a small circle and, more frequently, the renvers performed about one horse's length clear of the arena track so that the horse can be made to perform a half- or a three-quarter pirouette when he arrives at the corner, where the two walls will assist in the control (see Figure 11). Both these methods help to ensure that the rider has a high

Figure 11 *Pirouettes from canter renvers*

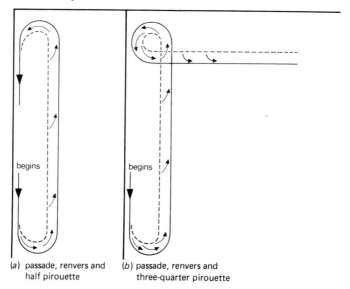

(a) passade, renvers and
half pirouette

(b) passade, renvers and
three-quarter pirouette

degree of control over his horse's quarters right up to the moment when the pirouette begins and, since that is so important, they have obvious attractions. But they also involve certain difficulties that can cause confusion at the crucial moment for less experienced riders, as we shall see. It will suffice for the moment to remind ourselves that neither travers nor renvers do anything to increase collection. Their purpose is chiefly that of activating, loosening and improving lateral control over the quarters.

It is vital in any half-pass, of which the pirouette is a form, that the quarters should not lead the forehand because, if they do, impulsion is gravely inhibited. The significance of that principle is at its greatest in the pirouette, where the degree of angle and general difficulty is most acute. To give the horse the best chance of discovering his ability to master this difficult exercise, we have to position the forehand correctly in relation to the quarters. If we get it wrong, we make it almost impossible for him to perform the movement at all competently.

Another point to remember in this connection is that the mechanics of a travers must not be confused with those of the half-pass. Those two movements, which at first sight have superficial similarities, are not at all the same thing. As can be seen from Figure 5 (page 64), the position of the quarters on their separate track in the travers will diminish, but not seriously jeopardize, the flow of impulsion through the horse into the rider's hands. That is so because the direction of movement and the direction of the flow of impulsion are almost identical.

The half-pass is a different matter altogether. It is much more difficult than the travers to do well, for both horse and rider, because the direction of movement bears little relation to the direction of the flow of impulsion (see Figure 5). Maintaining impulsion consequently presents considerable problems that do not exist to nearly the same extent in travers. If the quarters lead in the half-pass to any significant extent, impulsion will dwindle to zero and the movement will cease to be a half-pass. Ultimately, the horse will be going more and more sideways, rather than diagonally forwards and sideways. The distinction between these two movements – half-pass and travers – is of very real importance to the proper understanding of a pirouette.

The shoulder-in

We must now come to the crux of this part of the discussion and face up to the fact that, when it comes to the moment of truth and the pirouette itself, we should ride into it not out of a travers or a renvers, but out of a shoulder-in. The logic of this method is quite obvious. The shoulder-in is universally accepted as providing the ideal basis for a half-pass; it is the same for the pirouette because the latter, as we have seen, is a form of half-pass. The shoulder-in engenders impulsion and collection, whereas the travers does not. And the very essence of the shoulder-in lies in the fact that the forehand is placed in front of the haunches, thus forcing the inside hindleg to reach forward and under the horse's centre of gravity. From that position, the quarters can only assist, and cannot interfere with, the turning movement of the forehand. Conversely, if the pirouette is begun from a travers position, with the rider still trying to cause the quarters to move a little bit to the inside around the plate-sized circle, they will in effect be leading the forehand and will get in the way, positively inhibiting the latter's circular movement.

Looked at in another way, the circular movement of the forehand must dictate the speed of the turn, the quarters following just a fraction behind but in the same direction. Horse and rider will then be ready, at any moment, to initiate a controlled exit from the pirouette, on a straight line, slightly flexed to the inside in that faintly shoulder-in position that lies at the heart of a fully collected canter. The horse will have maintained the same position as he entered the pirouette, as he performed it, and as he left it. Performed in this manner, with all parts of the horse under perfect control, the pirouette becomes the ultimate example of the value of de la Guerinière's invention, the shoulder-in. The start may only be a suspicion of a shoulder-in, but it will be sufficient and it will work wonders. At this point it should hardly need saying that practising the canter shoulder-in should be one of the long-term preparatory exercises for the pirouette.

Small circles

It is not unusual to see riders preparing their horses for the pirouette by riding in small and decreasing one-track circles – presumably relying on the dubious theory that, when the circle becomes small enough, the horse will eventually and perforce have to lift his forehand around his quarters, the circle automatically converting itself into a kind of pirouette. This is an altogether fallacious theory and is, in addition, very bad psychology. The inexperienced horse will find it more and more difficult to keep himself in balance on the unduly small circle around which his rider is urging him and which he cannot possibly perform correctly on one track;

he will become flustered; he will lose rhythm and calmness; and he will in the end begin turning on his centre because he will be unable to prevent his quarters from flying out. The system, in short, is most likely to produce almost all the things that we most wish to avoid in pirouette work, and it cannot be too strongly deprecated.

Certainly the small canter circles can be used, within the normal limits of the classic volte of 6 metres diameter, to increase collection and improve the turning controls. Certainly the travers and renvers can be used to loosen and activate the hindlegs and to establish control of the quarters. But in the end it is the shoulder-in that has to be mastered, to however small a degree, before the rider can reasonably and safely ask his horse to perform even one step of the pirouette. Out of it the horse will progress with the all-important qualities of ease, confidence and calmness.

Sequence of work

We can now summarize the programme of work recommended for use by the relatively inexperienced rider in teaching the canter pirouette – all of it spread over at least several months depending on the talent, temperament and physical ability of the horse, and also of the rider. The special advantage claimed for the adoption of the sequence of work outlined here is that it virtually rules out the possibility of the young horse becoming excited or nervous of the strains that are imposed by pirouettes. He will quickly come to understand that the operation will always end quietly and before the stresses become acute. He will feel no urge to hurry and will know that his rider is not going to push, pull or hustle him beyond his capacity to obey in comfort. In short, the rider will retain his horse's confidence and consequently his co-operation. Mutual understanding will follow and smooth, steady progress can be made.

1   Collection

Work steadily and progressively to perfect the collection and the elasticity of the canter, to the point where the horse can perform two or three canter strides almost on the spot without loss of rhythm, always remaining on and up to the bit with a light contact and without stiffening. This work is best carried out on a large circle where the repetition can be frequent and where neither horse nor rider will be distracted by the constant negotiation of corners.

2   Walk to canter strike-off

Work to improve the collected and precision qualities of the canter strike-off from walk and, at the same time, of the downward transition from canter to walk. Aim to be able to do three, two, or even only one, collected canter strides out of a collected walk, terminating in a soft and equally collected transition back into walk – all to be executed with calmness and submission from the horse's back and mouth. The depart into only one canter stride is extremely difficult; it is probably beyond the capabilities of most riders and need not be insisted upon. Throughout this work the rider must insist that each strike-off is absolutely straight, both in the preceding walk and in the actual depart itself. It is even desirable to insist on a very slight shoulder-in effect during the whole process, not least because the pirouette, when we come to ask for it, is best begun from that same shoulder-in position, as already discussed. This exercise should also be practised as a half-pass right across the diagonal of the manège i.e. walk-canter-walk-canter, all in continuous half-pass.

3   Half-pass on a circle

Work in short spells of canter half-pass at first on a fairly large circle of 15 to 20 metres diameter but later reducing to 10 and eventually to about 7 or 8 metres. This work must be carried out in true half-pass form and not in a kind of travers. Travers would cause the horse to be too much bent overall and the direction of movement would be insufficiently sideways. Only if the horse positively seems to offer it, while remaining perfectly calm, should the rider be tempted at this stage to ask for anything resembling a true pirouette or even part of a pirouette, and even then the hindlegs should not, at this stage, be expected to move on a circle of less than a metre. Caution and patience at this stage will pay big dividends.

4   The seat

In all the work already described, the rider must concentrate, above all, on the stillness and perfection of his seat and leg position. Only the rider who can sit still and apply his aids in perfect balance in these and similar manoeuvres has the right to ask his horse for a pirouette. To do so without those qualities is unfair, unsightly and absurd.

5   *The first steps*

When the rider is satisfied that all these matters are going well, he can safely ask, immediately after a strike-off from a walk, for one, or at most two, turning strides of a fairly large pirouette of at least a metre diameter. As soon as he feels the required response from the horse, i.e. that the forehand turns while the quarters remain totally submissive to the control of the outside leg aid, he should immediately return to the walk by a direct transition and continue the pirouette movement for a further two or three steps in walk. This can be repeated several times, the horse remaining in collection throughout, before he is allowed to rest by walking forward with a loose rein and a pat on the neck. The purpose of continuing the pirouette in walk immediately after the downward transition is to teach the horse that he is expected to retain full control of himself and not to plunge forward on to his forehand as soon as he is released from the effort of the canter.

6   *The development*

As this work progresses, an improvement in the horse's readiness and ability to pick up into canter from a very collected walk will be noticeable. The rider will find it less and less difficult to re-start the canter into its pirouette-like sideways movement after each calming downward transition into walk. So, gradually and always calmly, it will become easy to increase the number of pirouette steps taken in succession, until a full half, three-quarter, or eventually whole, pirouette will be achieved. And, as this point approaches, it can be helpful to everyone's morale to continue occasionally for one and a half or two, or even three, full revolutions, provided that the moment seems appropriate and the horse does not have to be forced to do more steps than he can accomplish with ease. If the horse begins to feel tense or strained, the rider should acknowledge, almost with a sense of guilt, that he has asked for a step too many. The horse will thus learn that he may have to continue the pirouette for longer than he expected, and in any case must try to continue the movement until he is specifically released from it. But the rider is responsible for giving that release before rather than after the pirouette begins to suffer and crumble.

The rider, throughout the whole development period and later, must always see to it that he can ride straight forward out of the pirouette at any moment, without losing collection or breaking the rhythm, as an alternative to the transition into walk. This in itself needs much practice but is essential if full control is to be maintained. It is an exercise similar to the alternating half-pass and shoulder-in that is practised on straight lines.

The pivot theory

We have said that the quarters should act as the pivot of the arc around which the forehand has to move during a pirouette or part of a pirouette. In order to appreciate the full implication of that apparently simple statement it is necessary to look closely at the technicalities of exactly what the horse is required to do. These technicalities are very important if the movement is to be executed in classic form, and we cannot expect to train our horse correctly and efficiently unless we, the teachers, know precisely what we are trying to teach. We certainly cannot just leave it to the horse to do what he finds easiest, as that would end in allowing him to adopt his natural tendency to turn on his centre. We have to introduce him to a more sophisticated and more gymnastic method of turning.

It has become conventional to say that a pirouette should be performed round the pivot of the inside hindfoot. This is acceptable in a walk pirouette when the two hindfeet remain close together throughout the movement which is somewhat akin to a pirouette in piaffe, but it does not stand up to thorough analysis of the action required for a pirouette in canter. For the canter pirouette, the following distinctive factors have to be considered:

1   The inside hindfoot, at every stride, will be stepping well forward in advance of the outside hindfoot, towards the horse's centre of gravity, as is required in this gait for maximum collection and lightness of the forehand. If, in that forward position, the inside hindfoot were allowed to become the pivot of the turn, the horse would in effect be turning on his centre, the quarters swinging out to a greater or lesser extent according to the amount of collection achieved. But if the canter is true, this cannot in practice occur (see 2 below).

2   The inside hindleg never carries more than half the weight of the horse since it always shares the burden during a canter with its opposite or diagonal frontleg. Obviously a horse cannot pivot, or even turn at all, round two simultaneously-made footprints, one of them a front foot, some three feet apart on either end of a baseline that points outward from the circle.

3   There is no fixed or permanent pivot in a canter-pirouette because of the moment of suspension between each successive stride. A canter-pirouette therefore comprises six to eight quite distinct jump-turns to the side, each of approximately 50 degrees, forming separate segments of the whole circle and each with its own pivot.

4   It is the outside hindleg that initiates each successive canter stride or jump-turn, having returned to the ground on a fresh alignment for each one. It is the outside hindleg which, at that moment, carries the entire weight of the horse. And it is that outside hindleg that alone can thrust the horse sideways through the 50 degree turn (see page 96, half-passes; and photographs on pages 94 and 95); a turn that can only happen when the one hindleg is on the ground alone; a turn that ceases immediately a second and/or third leg also becomes grounded.

From those four considerations, it becomes clear that a full canter pirouette has a series of pivots, a fresh one for each of the segmental 50 degree turns that the horse has to make; and that each of the segmental turns will be based on, or pivot round, the outside hindleg that alone creates the turn and does all the work. In addition, the effect of the grounding of the inside hindleg is to stop the turn which can only recommence when the outside leg is once again alone on the ground.

To summarize, we have to conclude that:

a   The inside hindfoot will form the pivot of a pirouette in walk or piaffe.

b   The outside hindfoot forms the pivot of a correct and properly collected pirouette in canter.

In each case we accept that the pivot, as such, is mobile and intermittent.

Note: These conclusions, differing as they do from much contemporary writing, represent the author's personal convictions. But nevertheless they are amply endorsed by, among many others, the classic writer and Olympic rider Colonel Waldemar Seunig in his great book *Horsemanship*, (page 202).

For pirouette work in general, readers should also study General Decarpentry's teaching in *Academic Equitation* pages 204–208.

11

The Piaffe and the Passage

I commence this chapter with an expression of my considerable diffidence in writing on a subject of which my personal experience is comparatively limited. A few great horsemen with many years' experience and outstanding success in their achievements have made available their knowledge and advice in book form, and it would be impertinent of me to try to offer comparable opinions. Two authors in particular deal with the subject of the piaffe and the passage with admirable clarity and brevity, and all readers of this book are strongly recommended to read and study with close attention the relevant parts of *Reflections on Equestrian Art* by Nuno Oliveira and *Dressage Riding* by Richard Wätjen, both published in England by J. A. Allen. Both are excellently translated into English from the original French and German. There is very little of significance connected with the teaching of these two airs that is not at least implicit in those two expositions, and I shall not try here to duplicate or overlap their teaching. In both the text is complemented by many photographs that illustrate the movements to perfection. If it can be obtained, Hans Handler's *The Spanish Riding School* is also excellent on the subject.

Nevertheless, and since this book is written mainly for the relatively inexperienced rider who may be making his first assault on the higher peaks of equitation, there are some aspects of the study of piaffe and passage on which my opinion and experience may be of help to foster discussion and to dispel unnecessary fears.

When it comes to the point, neither the piaffe nor the passage will be created out of the thoughts, written or otherwise, of any teacher, but out of a mixture of the skill, knowledge and confidence of each rider. He must think and study until he acquires the confidence that he is doing the right thing, for the right reason, at the right time. Until that time arrives it is better to do nothing. Untidy ideas and intentions based on precipitate thought can only result in untidy aids, which in turn produce untidy results that may even jeopardize the hope of ultimately achieving a good piaffe. Better by far to begin with one small but clearly conceived step in the direction we want to go and, when that is consolidated, to move carefully forward to the next – each one being well within the compass of the current state of education of horse and rider. In that way, no harm will be done and some benefit will almost certainly accrue. So let everyone try. Any rider may find that his horse has considerable or even outstanding talent for the work so that progress comes unexpectedly quickly and easily.

The piaffe

Of all the movements that are developed, one from another, in the course of training a horse in the higher flights of dressage, the piaffe stands out from the others as requiring a rather different approach. The piaffe, it may be said, is merely the ultimate in collected trots, brought about by activating the quarters to the extent that the resulting impulsion can be directed perhaps 95 per cent upward and only 5 per cent forwards – that is, the trot is performed virtually on the spot. That may not sound very special or difficult, but in practice it is unexpectedly difficult for the horse to do. The plain fact of the matter is that only a quite small percentage of horses, however expertly trained, are able to produce a good and classically correct piaffe as and when required. A number may produce a reasonable interpretation of the movement on isolated occasions – when excited in the stable yard for instance, or when impatient on the way home from exercise, or even when warming up in the practice arena before a competition. But in many, many cases the spirit and the ability seem to ebb away when the piaffe is called for at some specified moment within the normal stresses and pressures of work, be it in competition or in a full-length display. Often, on such occasions, the much-vaunted piaffe is impossible to perform properly or is reduced to an unrhythmic shuffle.

The piaffe, like the flying change of leg, is something that the horse can often do by instinct and without the involvement of any intellectual processes. But the logic of it is hard for him to understand once he begins to think about it. Why should he try to trot when at the same time he is being asked to remain in the same place? It is usual for only one or two of the stallions in training at the Spanish Riding School in Vienna to be considered fit to show the piaffe in public exhibitions. And only about ten per cent of the entries at an Olympic contest will be really worth watching in piaffe. The difficulties are more likely to have a mental than a physical origin.

Nevertheless, we should not allow difficulties to make us timid. Every rider committed to training a dressage horse should certainly aim to include the piaffe in his repertoire, even if he only achieves it in a comparatively elementary form. The horse that refuses even to try a piaffe is clearly withholding something, and to that extent the rider will have to admit that he has failed to marshal all the forces at his disposal. He will not be master of his horse. And, even if the piaffe he achieves is of only modest proportions, its side-effects will nearly always improve the activity, engagement, impulsion and alertness that the horse subsequently shows in other work. But, in the end, the most pertinent question to be resolved is whether the rider rides well enough to create, without force, the activity of the quarters that initiates a piaffe. The movement is worth studying for that reason alone since mobilization of the hindquarters is the root of all dressage.

One of the peculiar distinctions of the piaffe is that, with very rare exceptions, it takes a long time, almost certainly several years, to develop this talent. It becomes quite obvious to the eye that most horses, even when they have begun to understand what they are being asked to do, find the whole thing a severe strain on their capabilities. Both physically and mentally, they take a long time to get accustomed to it, and the trainer must make appropriate allowances so as not to overtax their confidence and ability to co-operate.

The confidence of the horse is an important factor in teaching the piaffe, and the movement should be performed calmly, proudly and rhythmically. These qualities will never exist if the horse is nervous, stressful, anxious or just physically weak. Progress should always be made with discretion, steadily and without haste, until the time eventually comes when the horse will accept the work with ease and will be able to offer the movement generously. In most cases, the first gentle introduction to the piaffe can be safely made quite early in the training programme, or as soon as the horse has learnt to show real collection and to go powerfully forward, in both cases with submission.

Definition

The internationally accepted definition of the piaffe is worth quoting for its clarity.

1   The piaffe is a highly measured, collected, elevated and cadenced trot on the spot. The horse's back is supple and vibrating. The quarters are slightly lowered, the haunches with active hocks are well engaged, giving great freedom, lightness and mobility to the shoulders and forehand. Each diagonal pair of feet is raised and returned to the ground alternately, with an even rhythm and a slightly prolonged suspension.

(Comment: All authorities do not agree about the prolonged period of suspension. In practice, it is seldom noticeable, and the late Colonel Hans Handler states, in his book The Spanish Riding School, *'of all the different kinds of trot, the piaffe has the shortest moment of suspension'. Colonel Handler states that the haunches should be 'deeply bent'.)*

2   In principle, the height of the toes of the raised foreleg should be level with the middle of the canon bone of the other foreleg. The toe of the raised hindleg should reach just above the fetlock joint of the other hindleg.

(Comment: The hindfeet should not – and if the haunches are appropriately lowered they cannot – be raised as high as the front feet.)

3   The neck should be raised and arched, the head perpendicular. The horse should remain light 'on the bit' with a supple poll, maintaining a light contact on a taut rein. The body of the horse should move up and down in a supple, cadenced and harmonious movement.

(Comment: If the horse is not on the bit, with supple poll and head perpendicular, the back will not be supple and vibrating, and the quarters will not lower.)

4   The piaffe, though executed strictly on the spot and with perfect balance, must always be animated by a lively impulsion which is displayed in the horse's constant desire to move forward as soon as the aids for the piaffe cease.

(Comment: The horse must never appear, or be allowed, to drift to the rear, nor should the hocks appear to move backwards as they lift the feet from the ground. The requirement for the horse to remain strictly on the spot has not always been specified, and a slight forward progression of about 1 metre in six or eight steps should certainly be demanded in the early stages of training, to ensure and demonstrate that the horse is working up to the bit and maintaining his essential urge to go forward.)

The four paragraphs just quoted, together with the short chapters on the piaffe in the books recommended at the beginning of this discussion, give ample evidence of the complexities of the movement. They should be studied with the utmost care and attention to detail before any work on the piaffe is begun. They contain all the key points, but there are certain

A piaffe that is very good throughout the forehand, with excellent elevation of the fore-leg, the neck long and unconstrained. The quarters are nicely lowered but the hind feet have come too far forward in front of a vertical line through the stifle, thus engendering tension in the hocks and making it difficult for the horse to thrust himself off the ground with the required suspension and cadence, and making elevation of the hind feet almost impossible. Reiner Klimke on Fabian

aspects that I would like to underline, by way of assisting the beginner who does not have ready access to expert advice.

Collection

The collection, and consequently the whole piaffe, must emanate from regulated activity of the haunches and hindlegs, which must therefore be

A very fine piaffe by Nuno Oliveira on a Lusitanian stallion. Hind feet have come a little too far forward but there is no tension and the hocks flex easily to produce excellent elevation of the hind feet. The face is vertical on a very light contact. The poll is at the highest point, the neck long, the back rounded and supple, the horse totally calm and relaxed.

A fairly good piaffe. The raised front cannon should be nearer to the vertical and a little higher (see photographs on pages 132 and 133). Quarters nicely lowered and engaged with active and well flexed hocks, showing excellent balance. The poll is fractionally too low and the neck rather short. Horse shows no tension and remains supple, active and keen. Jennie Loriston-Clarke on Dutch Courage

brought into a position that will allow the impulsion they generate to lift the body upwards with each diagonal step. The forehand must clearly become much lighter than the quarters, and for this it is mechanically essential that the haunches be lowered and the hindfeet brought further forward under the body mass than is necessary for any other movement so far attempted. But, in doing this, care must be taken that the horse is not encouraged to bring his hindfeet forward to the extent that he is no longer able to flex the joints sufficiently to deliver the upward thrust. The ideal position for the hindfeet will be more or less vertically under the stifle joint.

Any tendency for the croup to become higher than the withers, instead of lowering, is very bad and must not be tolerated. Such a posture means that the quarters are doing nothing to take weight off the forehand which will remain more or less rooted to the ground. It is thus the very antithesis of collection.

Trouble will result if the horse is allowed, at the beginning, to form the habit of moving his feet in a trot sequence without making any effort to lower and engage the quarters. In such a case, when an increase of energy is requested, the hindlegs are likely to become even more disengaged, the hocks even appearing to lift upwards and backwards from the ground. To make matters worse, the quarters, not being loaded, will leave the forehand to carry its own weight, with the result that the forelegs will show less elevation and suspension than the hindlegs, instead of more. The croup will probably rise with each step in a bumpy manner. In short, the horse is in no way collected and is not complying with the fundamental requirements of a piaffe.

Alternative approaches

The early lessons of work in piaffe can be taught either from the ground, referred to as 'work-in-hand', or mounted, from the saddle.

From the ground: The dismounted work-in-hand is perhaps the most fashionable and is practised, though not exclusively, at the Spanish Riding School. It can, however, involve considerable difficulty for the trainer who has to work alone or without a properly enclosed manège. Some horses become excited and very difficult to control, and in those circumstances the exercise can easily end in trouble and frustration.

Logically, there is much to be said in favour of at least some initial work-in-hand, not least because it gives the horse the chance to learn to overcome the basic problems of the piaffe without the encumbrance of a rider on his back. And, as in lunge work, it is of great value for the trainer, especially when working alone and without mirrors, to be able to understand exactly how his horse is reacting in his eyes as well as with his limbs. The principles of work-in-hand for piaffe are admirably set out in *Dressage Riding* by Richard Wätjen, pages 90–99, and need no further elaboration.

A fairly good piaffe with active hindlegs. A slight loss of impulsion shows in the very light contact on the bridoon rein, and in the withdrawal of the raised forefoot

It is also possible to do useful preparatory work by driving the horse in long reins; but here again it is advisable at the outset to have help from an assistant who leads the horse by a short rein. One of the dangers of working the piaffe in long reins ensues from the difficulty of controlling the elevation and the bend of the neck and poll with the result that the horse is liable to produce a piaffe that is croup high. Once started this fault will be very difficult to cure.

From the saddle: There are many experienced trainers who prefer to work from the outset from the saddle – among them the Portuguese master, Nuno Oliveira, probably the most prolific producer of the classic piaffe alive today. His *Reflections on Equestrian Art* is of very great value over the

A good piaffe, the improved impulsion producing a better verticality of the raised fore-leg, and leaving the poll clearly the highest point of the neck. Hocks properly flexed and active, with quarters lowered. Rider's hands unnecessarily high. Good back and leg positions, without reliance on the spur. Jaqueline Farlow on Snap Happy

whole range of the *haute école*, and he deals with the piaffe most lucidly on pages 76, 79 and 80.

One advantage of the mounted method is that the work can be introduced into the training programme, and into the horse's mind, almost without his noticing it, and without the creation of the special and possibly rather alarming atmosphere of a piaffe session with short side reins, cavessons and assistants with long whips. Work from the saddle can be slipped into the daily routine whenever the moment seems appropriate – at the beginning of the morning when the horse is fresh, or later when he is well put to the aids, or at the end of the workout just before he is released from school, or with variations. In any case, there will be the minimum disturbance or inconvenience for all concerned.

But perhaps the most important benefit of teaching the piaffe from the saddle is that the exercise will then be taught, from the very beginning, with the use of precisely the same aids. Furthermore, they will be the aids that the horse has been taught to accept and respond to from the earliest days of his education, whenever an increase of activity or of collection has been required. And, since the piaffe is founded on activity and collection, it must be logical to continue to employ those same aids, not to lose faith in them, and not to break the horse's confidence in them by suddenly asking for those same reactions with a different set of aids and equipment. It is also easier to keep the horse straight from the saddle.

In the end, each trainer must make his own choice of the method to adopt for the early lessons, his decision being very largely influenced by the facilities available to him and the amount of experienced assistance he can call upon. Quite satisfactory results may be obtained by either method, provided the trainer combines firmness, intelligence and patience, and makes full use of the advice available to him in the books already mentioned. However, we will assume that the rider, working alone, will teach the exercise from the saddle.

Aids for the piaffe

The piaffe is the ultimate in collection and activity in trot. The aids to be employed must therefore be a braced but supple back enlivening a deep, still seat with downward-stretching legs that murmur encouragement to the horse with the minimum of disturbance or movement. The body above the waist does nothing, and the hands must be delicately light and very still.

With the piaffe, as with the passage, it is more than ever important that the rider should be absolutely consistent and precise with his aids. Both these movements share certain characteristics connected with cadence and upward impulsion that are not found in any other pace or movement in the various trots. And yet, on the face of it, the rider is still only asking for collection and impulsion, with aids that must obviously be appropriate for those qualities. He has therefore to face the question of how he can make it clear to the horse that he is asking for a piaffe, or a passage (which is closely related), rather than for any normal form of trot. This does not mean that the aids for these two movements are derived from some kind of magic touch, but it does mean that the logic of the aid alphabet that has already been established must be developed and refined to a high state of finesse, and then adhered to meticulously. The need for finesse will be especially felt when it comes to performing with unbroken rhythm the transitions direct from the piaffe into the passage and then back from passage to piaffe.

The aids will also have to cater for transitions from piaffe to collected trot or collected walk, and from passage direct into, say, a medium or extended trot or into a canter. A very refined and subtle language has to be built up between horse and rider to make these things possible. This requires intelligent horsemanship and some years of practice.

No two riders' aids can be precisely similar, because of their inevitable differences in physiology. To some extent, therefore, each and every rider must discover for himself, in co-operation with his horse, the niceties of these refined aids. But, for those riders who have not previously tackled these problems, the following suggestions may be helpful.

The rider's prime purpose is to activate and engage the horse's hindlegs, but without asking for, or allowing, any significant forward movement. Both his legs may therefore be positioned a little further back on the horse's flank or rib cage than normal, so that they are clearly not in the forward-urging position on the girth. Once in position, there should be no to-and-fro movement of the legs, which should remain steadily in contact with the horse, well stretched down into the heels to complement the strong bracing of the back that constitutes the main influence on the horse. If possible, the required reaction from the horse should be obtained without the use, and certainly without the constant use, of the spur. The rider's buttocks should remain open, and the inside of the thigh, knee and calf should retain contact with the horse. If additional stimulation is needed, the heels can be turned in with a light, rhythmical movement to bring the spur into gentle contact without diminishing or altering the aid of the leg itself.

The fact that the legs should be well stretched down is not, of course, peculiar to the piaffe. The lowered heel, which implies a lengthened leg, should be an essential part of any form of leg aid, forward or lateral, for the good reason that it makes the aid more effective. The importance of this aspect of the rider's performance can hardly be overestimated, least of all in trying to ride a piaffe. The heel should not, however, be forced down so that the ankle becomes fixed and rigid.

Since we have already given some thought to the problems confronting the horse in executing the piaffe, it will come as no surprise to discover the difficulties it presents to the rider. He has to create something tremendous out of virtually nothing (a piaffe from a halt or a walk) and he has to do it without delay or hesitation, without apparent effort, and with elegance, feeling and tact. Poor piaffes can be, and frequently are, created with much accentuated and even violent movement from the rider's body (as if it was he who had to bounce up and down); this may also come from his hands (like those of the costermonger who creates action from his donkey by jerking the reins), or from his legs (as if he were attacking a refusing horse). These eccentricities are a mockery of real horsemanship and the sort of piaffe that they may produce is of little value or interest, notably because it is bound to be given unwillingly. It will also be uncomfortable and will lack pride and rhythm.

The rider must, if his horse is to perform with comfort and contentment, keep his body and hands absolutely still and his hips and stomach thrust well forward, and he must maintain a strong but supple back and loins that will feel, encourage and steady the movement flowing from the horse's quarters in response to his aids. It is this combination of aids that holds the key to success, because the piaffe depends above all on the degree to which the rider has already trained his horse to respond in a generous, round and supple manner to the combined aids of loins, seat and legs.

The passage

There is no hard-and-fast rule about whether the piaffe should be taught before the passage, or vice versa. On balance, however, there is a greater weight of opinion on the side of teaching the piaffe first, mainly because of the danger that, having learnt the passage first, the horse will thereafter always tend to make too much use of the powerful forward thrust from the quarters that he has learnt, and so find it difficult to learn to adopt the more sitting posture that is required for the piaffe. The inexperienced trainer should therefore beware of the fact that, though it is probably easier to teach a little passage than a little piaffe, he may quite possibly, by teaching the easier one first, be effectively precluding himself from ever achieving a piaffe. That may sound paradoxical and contrary to the general principles of equitation, but it deserves consideration.

Evasion

There is also another danger. If the passage is introduced too early, before the horse is totally reliable in his obedience and responsiveness to subtle

A passage with excellent elevation in front but modest behind. Note the unconstrained neck with the poll at the highest point. Note also the rider's excellent seat and pelvic position. Reiner Klimke on Ahleric

variations of the aids, and particularly to the aids for collection and impulsion, he will be liable to fall into passage when the rider has only asked for trot. He may genuinely have misunderstood the request, but it is also quite likely that he will use the passage-like steps as an evasion of the effort required to produce the strong forward impulsion required for the normal trot. Once this latter trick of evasion has been learnt, it will be extremely annoying and difficult to eradicate.

In theory, there should be at least as much genuine impulsion in a passage as in any other movement, but in practice, because the impulsion

A well engaged passage with even and fairly good elevation, showing slight shortening and overbending in the neck, the poll coming too low. Rider a little in front of the movement. Jennie Loriston-Clarke on Dutch Courage

is directed more upwards than forwards, the rider will usually be only too pleased if he has obtained his early passage steps with a degree of rein contact that he would in other circumstances have considered insufficient. The horse therefore learns that, in passage, he can to some extent come off the bit and get away with it, and it is that knowledge that he will make use of, to his own advantage, when ignoring the rider's demands for fully forward impulsion. If that begins to happen it may be necessary to reprimand him promptly and smartly with whip or spur, making it quite plain that such reaction will not be tolerated. That is one good reason for postponing the introduction of the passage until quite late in the horse's education – whereas some tactful approach to the piaffe can be made relatively early with very little danger and with quite considerable benefit to general progress in other paces.

Despite its dangers, the passage is an elegant and pleasurable movement that must be regarded as an essential part of the repertoire of every fully trained dressage horse and rider. It must, at the appropriate time, be tackled, and the reader is again recommended to study the excellently brief writings of Nuno Oliveira and Richard Wätjen for the details of how best to do it. To those writings the author can add nothing except perhaps a few words about the aids for passage as distinct from those for piaffe.

Aids for the passage

We have already suggested that, for the piaffe, the rider's legs should be positioned a little further back than normal because they are not going to ask for actual forward movement beyond that of the basic impulsive urge; they are concentrating on the activity and engagement of the haunches, thus making it easier for the horse to understand the rider's instructions. For the passage, we want maximum impulsion or thrust but this time about equally divided between the upward and the forward directions. For this, the rider's legs will need to act on the girth in the normal position, but in a somewhat different manner.

If the legs are activated in the on-the-girth position with frequent and recurrent quick applications of pressure, the horse is entitled to think that he is being asked to increase his forward speed, which would result in a lengthening of the stride if the reins allowed it, or possibly in a quickening of the tempo. Neither of these reactions helps towards the achievement of a passage and something else is required to induce a totally different form of action – something that the horse will not have experienced before and

A satisfactory passage with excellent engagement and elevation of the hindleg. Horse remains relaxed with correct outline of neck and poll. Very good position of the rider with loins supple and well braced to absorb and direct the movement. Jaqueline Farlow on Snap Happy

can consequently be reserved for the passage only, thus obviating the dangers of misunderstanding or error that we have already discussed. This special form of aid can be found, without violating any of the previously established principles, if the rider lengthens his legs to the maximum, endeavouring to wrap them round and under his horse, and then exerts a steady, prolonged and simultaneous pressure from both legs that 'stays on' for at least the duration of one whole stride.

The prolonged pressure of both legs must, it should go without saying, be accompanied and complemented by a co-ordinated bracing of the back. The wrap-round leg pressure induces the horse to lift his body

In this passage a slight flattening of the back has resulted in an increased extension of the forearm and rather less elevation. The rider again shows a correct position. Jaqueline Farlow on Snap Happy

further upwards than usual, and is carefully timed and repeated with each step, though without ever being totally removed. It also helps the rider to keep his seat absolutely still in contact with the saddle throughout the increased rise and fall of the movement, which must tend to throw the rider and to be more than usually difficult to sit through. If the rider's back is not sufficiently strong and supple to cope with this problem, he will inevitably bump in the saddle and thus disturb and discomfort his horse, discouraging him from making the supreme effort required of his own back.

If the rider cannot sit through the elevation of the passage, particularly in the early stages when the horse has still to acquire confidence in his

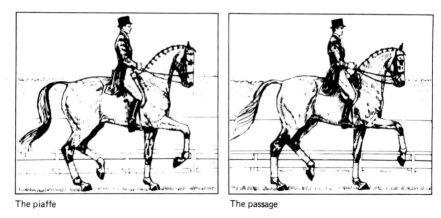

The piaffe   The passage

Figure 12 *Artist's drawing of an excellent piaffe and passage* (by Patricia Frost)

ability to perform the movement, the hands will not be still and the horse
will be interfered with in his mouth as well as in his back. So once again it
is a matter of: rider, perfect thyself before thy horse.

Transitions

When the passage and the piaffe have been mastered individually and can
be performed by the horse with comparative ease and confidence with the
use only of discreet aids, it will be time to put the two airs together and to
practise riding each of them directly out of the other. The major problem
with these transitions is how to make them smoothly, without break or
change in the rhythm; the solution lies in the maintenance of unbroken
impulsion throughout the process of adjustment of the aids from one
movement to the other. If the steadiness of the impulsion is affected by an
abrupt change of aids, or if the aids for the second movement are applied
more violently than those for the first, it is obvious that the horse will
react abruptly and that the rhythm of the transition will consequently
be broken. It follows that the key to ultimate success in these transitions
lies in the perfection of control and precision by the rider of his own
aids.

These transitions are very difficult and demand a high level of training,
co-operation and performance from both horse and rider, The horse is
operating under extreme pressure in piaffe and in passage, and the smallest
flaw in balance at any stage of the process will render a good transition

impossible. This places a tremendous responsibility upon the rider. It is he who decides exactly when the transition is to be made, and he must ensure that his own balance and poise, contact with the bit and leg control are well-nigh perfect. It is the horse, not the rider, who makes the piaffe and the passage, but it is usually the rider who makes or mars the transition.

Passage with excellent elevation in front but insufficient engagement and activity behind, the raised toe being barely as high as the coronet. Christine Stuckelberger on Granat

Summary

Teaching the piaffe from the saddle is a perfectly practicable proposition for any reasonably talented rider. For such a rider, working alone, it is not necessarily any more difficult to obtain at least a modest piaffe than it is to teach flying changes of leg, and probably a good deal easier than it is to obtain consistent one-time changes. The mounted method can be thoroughly recommended, and the following outline of how to proceed may be helpful.

Piaffe programme

a   Teach the horse to trot actively but very slowly, with maintained impulsion on a very light contact. He must respond instantly to impulsive demands from the back-seat-legs.

Note: This may not be as easy as it sounds, and the lesson may take a week or more. Hitherto the horse has been made to trot always with powerful forward impulsion and with fairly long, flowing strides. Now he has to learn that that type of trot is not always required and must adapt himself to a quite different style.
b   Practise transitions from collected walk into the slow trot, and then from the halt into the slow trot, always with light contact, a steady head and with impulsion.
c   Practise transitions from the halt into a trot that barely moves forward, but do not yet think about piaffe.
d   Practise many transitions halt-trot-halt-trot, with slight forward movement.

When these exercises can be done calmly and with complete submission, the horse will begin to offer a true piaffe in response to aids applied equally calmly but very positively, the back being braced very strongly in a somewhat downward or static manner and the legs stretching down and closing firmly at a position somewhat behind the normal position for trot-on. The rider should expect to obtain the response without the use of the spur, which should only very occasionally be brought into play.
    The rider should particularly bear in mind:

e   The back-seat-leg aids should be quiet, firm and well coordinated.
f   Rein-aids only sufficient to prevent excessive forward movement, leaning on the bit, or the horse throwing himself on his forehand.

g   Only a very few piaffe steps should be asked for at a time during the first few months of this work, so as not to overtax the muscles and thereby cause mental anxiety.

h   The smallest success must regularly be acknowledged with neck-pats.

i   The upper body must be kept still, leaving the horse to make his own piaffe without disturbance.

j   Never allow the horse to anticipate the piaffe, and do not practise it for too long each day. Intersperse it with loose-rein walk and trot. It must never become a stress-movement.

Addendum

Since this book was published, veterinary science has shown conclusively that no lateral bend or flexion can be obtained from that part of the horse's spine behind thoracic vertebra 13 i.e. approximately the point on which the rider sits. Some of the line drawings in the book are consequently not strictly accurate in this respect. The wording of the main text, however, reflects the new knowledge.

The End
The author on Valentine

Index